PROFESS
SERVICE ACROSS
THE FIELD OF
EDUCATION
GUIDELINES FOR PARTICIPATION

Service is increasingly recognized as a crucial part of academic life, and in this incredibly competitive industry, trustworthy best practice guides are notably missing. Even with supportive mentors, many emergent scholars are left to learn these lessons the hard way. In this straightforward and thorough book, Joy Egbert and Mary Roe address the most common challenges facing academics at all stages of their careers as they navigate the world of professional service.

Illuminating the unspoken rules behind book reviewing, anticipating the difficulties of collaborating, offering support on chairing, mentoring, and graduate student committee chairing, and more, this book is a must-have for anyone starting an academic career in education and for veteran academics who want to polish their skills.

Joy Egbert is Professor in the Department of Teaching and Learning at Washington State University, Pullman.

Mary F. Roe is Professor and Department Head for the School of Teacher Education and Leadership at Utah State University, Logan.

PROFESSIONAL SERVICE ACROSS THE FIELD OF EDUCATION

GUIDELINES FOR PARTICIPATION

JOY EGBERT

MARY F. ROE

Routledge
Taylor & Francis Group

NEW YORK AND LONDON

First published 2016
by Routledge
711 Third Avenue, New York, NY 10017

and by Routledge
2 Park Square, Milton Park, Abingdon, Oxon, OX14 4RN

Routledge is an imprint of the Taylor & Francis Group, an informa business

© 2016 Taylor & Francis

The right of Joy Egbert and Mary F. Roe to be identified as authors of this work
has been asserted by them in accordance with sections 77 and 78 of the Copyright,
Designs and Patents Act 1988.

All rights reserved. No part of this book may be reprinted or reproduced or utilised in
any form or by any electronic, mechanical, or other means, now known or hereafter
invented, including photocopying and recording, or in any information storage or
retrieval system, without permission in writing from the publishers.

Trademark notice: Product or corporate names may be trademarks or registered
trademarks, and are used only for identification and explanation without intent to
infringe.

Library of Congress Cataloging-in-Publication Data
Names: Egbert, Joy, author. | Roe, Mary F., author.
Title: Professional service across the field of education : guidelines
    for participation / Joy Egbert and Mary F. Roe.
Description: New York : Routledge, 2016. | Includes bibliographical references.
Identifiers: LCCN 2015036582 | ISBN 9781138920804 (hardback) |
    ISBN 9781138920811 (pbk.) | ISBN 9781315686813 (ebook)
Subjects: LCSH: College teachers—Vocational guidance. | College
    administrators—Vocational guidance. | Scholars—Vocational guidance.
Classification: LCC LB1778 .E449 2016 | DDC 378.1/2—dc23
LC record available at http://lccn.loc.gov/2015036582

ISBN: 978-1-138-92080-4 (hbk)
ISBN: 978-1-138-92081-1 (pbk)
ISBN: 978-1-315-68681-3 (ebk)

Typeset in Minion and Scala Sans
by Apex CoVantage, LLC

For Princess and Super Pickle: always, and everything. And to Mary Roe, friend, colleague, co-conspirator, and role model for all things professional.

—J.E.

To the many personal friends and professional colleagues whose everyday lives indicate their commitment to service.

—M.F.R.

Contents

Teachers, higher education faculty, administrators, parents, students, and even community members participate in service to education. Some of these participants are required to do a certain amount of service, and some serve out of sheer generosity. Service to the field of education includes a large array of opportunities, and each level of education has its own needs. This text provides information for those in higher education, although many of the ideas and guidelines can be used by stakeholders at other levels.

The purpose of this text is to support those who want to participate at any level and might not be aware of many of the opportunities or might not understand how to go about participating in those opportunities. Ward (2010) notes that "the service role tends to be misunderstood, ill-defined, and often unrewarded" (p. 59) and, as she states, "if faculty are uncertain about the service component of their jobs, to their graduate students it often remains a mystery" (p. 58). We believe that education needs all the support it can get, and so this text addresses a variety of opportunities for service to the profession by all its stakeholders.

During our many years of teaching and working as higher education faculty, we have participated (more than once) in each of the opportunities in this text. This text is based both on our extensive experience and also on information from the education literature. We intend this book to be both a resource for education students and a reminder for those with more experience of the need for and essentials of service.

ACKNOWLEDGMENTS

The authors wish to thank Rebecca Novack, Routledge editor and the easiest person to work with *ever*, for her constant support and enthusiasm. It is always a pleasure! We also express our gratitude for mentors who have facilitated our service to education throughout our careers and to our students who carry on with service with amazing zeal.

1

SERVICE TO THE PROFESSION

From a faculty annual review summary paragraph about service:

This year I coordinated the development of 6 new online classes for the endorsement and completed numerous activities as Programs Coordinator. Seven of my graduate students finished this year and I still have 7 doctoral students. I had hundreds of meetings last year, serving from Global Campus to the Provost's Office to coordinating programs in the department. In addition, I received a number of small grants to support innovative practice with the group that I coordinate. I presented an invited symposium to the Department of Foreign Languages, a presentation with a local colleague at the technology conference on campus, and two forums at my field's international conference. I guest edited an issue of a journal in my field and reviewed over 2 dozen manuscripts for disciplinary journals. Additional service includes:

- Liaison for Fulbright Scholar
- College International Committee member and International Days coordinator

- Member of doctoral committee at an international university
- External reviewer for three promotion and tenure candidates

Overview

This excerpt shows just a sample of the types of professional service in which faculty, staff, and students can participate. Not everyone will provide the same types of service, nor should they; in this text, we encourage potential service providers to work in their areas of expertise and interest. That said, however, we also encourage readers to explore types of service they had not previously considered and think about whether there are other areas in which their service could provide benefit to themselves, their institution, and/or their profession.

This chapter introduces the following topics:

- Overview of service
  o What "service" is
  o The importance of service in education
- Using this text
  o Assumptions about service
  o Description of this text

Exploring the Idea of Service in Education

Members of many higher education communities, including faculty, staff, and students, are compelled for a variety of reasons to participate in service activities; however, often only a loose common understanding exists about what constitutes service in those communities. Across institutions the term is even less clear, perhaps in part because it is difficult to make a list of service activities that everyone can agree to. As Ward (2003) explains, the meaning of service, "for whom, and how it is rewarded remains unclear because service roles within higher education are not clearly defined and because people mean different things when they talk about faculty service" (iii). Her assertion is supported by service documents from across higher education. For example, UC-Berkeley's (2007) *Guidelines for Evaluation of Service in Faculty Performance Review* "are intended to provide a framework for how service is to be evaluated; they are not prescriptive" (p. 1). In other words, it is up to the faculty member to figure out how to serve. In a similar vein, UT-Chattanooga's (2013) document states that "Specific service expectations will be negotiated by the faculty member and the department head" (p. 1); this implies that "what counts" might be different for everyone. This trend toward ambiguity continues at Texas Christian University (TCU, 2012), with faculty noting that "Although there is a definite expectation that faculty members will be involved in service, this is the single cohesive element that exists between these service policies" (p. 2). Because of the amorphous nature of service across the profession, it is only possible to generate a general description of what it is. This broad definition is presented in what follows and provides the foundation for the information in this text.

What "Service" Is

Some authors have attempted to define service by creating general categories into which it might fit. For example, Ward (2003) parses service into internal and external categories, noting that internal service is service to the institution and external service operates in contexts beyond the campus. UC-Berkeley (2007) even suggests that there is "nonstandard service," which is

ambiguous with respect to how it should be considered. For example, the following situations may not be clear as to whether the contribution is to research, teaching, or service: (1) directing a field program overseas, which involves administrative service while at the same time contributing to one's research activities; or (2) administering an exchange program, where the faculty member directs the program while also teaching students in the program.

(p. 4)

Further, Comerford (2014) differentiates public service from professional and institutional service, suggesting that all three are essential to the mission of higher education. In addition, some service might be invited and some competitive, while other can be compulsory—for example, serving on department committees might be required—and still other is volunteer. We propose in this text that these categories are not mutually exclusive; for example, a federal curriculum development grant that brings money and positions to the campus (internal service), results in brown-bag presentations or other sharing within and outside the institution (internal and public service), *and* addresses the needs of an external population by providing a curriculum for schools in Afghanistan (public/external service) can have aspects of all these categories.

The diverse parameters noted above seem to work against a cohesive definition of the term "service." Because there are already many perspectives on what constitutes service, in this text we do not differentiate or categorize types of service in any evaluative way. Rather, in this book we regard all types of professional service as one outgrowth of the academic and administrative endeavors that take place in higher education. Ward (2003) agrees that "[service] is a way for faculty to apply their disciplinary expertise" (p. v), and we add that it is also a way for administrative staff to become involved in applications of their knowledge and experience. Therefore, for the purposes of this text, we suggest that *in serving, faculty and staff provide knowledge and/or skills based in their expertise, and they share with a variety of audiences resources that are integrated with their research, teaching, and/or administrative understandings.* This general definition fits all the types of service described in this text and allows those who serve not only to choose how to do so but also to decide on the relative worth of their service.

Importance of Service in Education

In addition to teaching and research, service is seen by both the general public and higher education institutions as an essential component of what higher education does. In part this importance comes from the history of higher education and from political, economic, and workplace perspectives (for more information on these issues, see Chambers, 2005; Mendoza & Gardner, 2010). While an exhaustive list of specific benefits from all the service that faculty, staff, and students do would take a book itself, general benefits are easy to note. For faculty, Comerford (2014) notes that "service not only allows for and encourages different forms of creative and professional expression, but also provides new opportunities to learn and teach. As such, it is an integral aspect of educational life" (p. 1). In addition, service can provide new perspectives to many audiences, and it might allow for collaborations that undercut the "ivory tower" perception of higher education some stakeholders might have. Furthermore, service can provide funding and other support for groups within and outside the university, facilitating change. It can also help faculty, staff, and others make links between theory and practice and connections among themselves through professional networking. Finally, participating in service activities can provide models for our students of how they might participate in society in ways that benefit both themselves and others.

Using This Text

This text focuses on helping readers understand various service forums and provides guidelines for how to perform various aspects of service. However, before using this text, we have several assumptions we expect readers to have considered.

Assumptions About Service

First, we suggest that service that is not done well, like many other things in life, is probably not worth doing. To that end, we expect that all service will be performed up to or exceeding the stakeholders' expectations, including language use, writing style, time spent, interaction, record keeping, or whatever else pertains. In addition, we leave the relevance of the service up to the person who decides to serve. We expect that the service is based on both expertise and interest, and since the content of most of the types of service we discuss is open, we leave it up to the server to choose what kind of service to participate in. In the same way, we hope that careful thought and planning will go into the service; faculty members, staff, and students who take on too much service, in addition to other responsibilities, might not be effective at any of it.

Finally, we assume that all stakeholders will work toward rectifying the issues that Comerford (2014, n.p.) discusses; she reminds us that

> Service is an aspect of academic life which is never taught in a classroom, though it is required. Perhaps the reason for this is that we expect our colleagues to have a service mentality, to assume responsibilities not only within the classroom but outside as well. On the positive side, this attitude allows for a great deal of variety in the kinds of acceptable service, and encourages self-starters. On the negative side, it means that institutional and professional statements explaining the purpose of service are rare.

To begin to close the gaps Comerford mentions, the following list, adapted from Ward (2010), recommends specific actions to help graduate students become more aware of service; we suggest that faculty and staff can also benefit from her recommendations:

- Invite faculty/staff who work at different types of institutions to talk about their service role.

- Present faculty/staff work topics in the community.
- Bring colleagues and students in on service activities.
- Exemplify how faculty/staff document their service work.
- Review reward structures, including paperwork from faculty/staff who have successfully presented their work.
- Appoint students to relevant committees.
- Provide support for students to participate in professional organizations.
- Review faculty dossiers so students can see how service fits in.

Working through this book with colleagues and students might also help programs or departments develop an appropriate reward structure for service and support collaboration in service endeavors.

Description of This Text

The purpose of this book, then, is to help readers choose and carry out service, understand benefits of each type of service mentioned, and think beyond what others are doing to new ways to serve. This book can be read in order from start to finish, or it can be used to look up ideas about ways to serve and how to do so. We have chosen the most common forms of service to address in this text; as noted previously, by no means is this an exhaustive list. Additional suggestions for types of service are presented throughout. Chapter topics and a short explanation of each follow:

- Chapter 2: Presentations (competitive, in-service, etc.)
  Ward (2010) notes that "the dissemination element of research plays an important role in communicating research findings beyond a particular campus setting" (p. 61). Presenting at conferences and in other forums is one of the most common and useful ways of sharing understandings, but figuring out what to present and how to do so can be difficult.

- Chapter 3: Reviewing manuscripts
  Many faculty and administrators serve as manuscript reviewers for one or more journals in the field. This common service work benefits reviewers not only by keeping them up on new developments in the field but also by helping them understand issues with research and writing.

- Chapter 4: Writing reviews of published academic books, trade books, and media
  Graduate students and new faculty often start their reviewing service by performing reviews of materials that may not have the same kinds of deadlines journal articles might and that they may be more familiar with. However, guidelines for this kind of reviewing are different from those for reviewing research articles.

- Chapter 5: Arranging collaborative action research
  Collaborative research across levels and disciplines that focuses on classroom teachers' needs can be one of the most effective service applications in obtaining specific and useful results.

- Chapter 6: Administrative service
  Ward (2010) notes that "Because of the nature of faculty meetings and departmental decision making, students typically are not privy to the inner workings of faculty service on campus, and they rarely witness faculty involvement in disciplinary service" (p. 64). Although some aspects of internal governance are limited to faculty and staff in specific positions, there are ways for students to participate. For example, doctoral students could be part of search committees, scholarship-granting committees, meetings for teaching groups, and others. However, attending is not generally enough—involvement in this work is important.

- Chapter 7: Mentoring students
  Ward (2010) notes that "Typically, direct advising of students falls under the rubric of teaching (although it certainly has a service element)" (p. 63). We believe, however, that good advising is a major service not only to the student but also to the campus community and the profession. Often students mentor each other, too, and guidelines can help this mentoring be effective.

- Chapter 8: Providing internal and external professional development
  Faculty, staff, and students at all levels can participate in rewarding and useful professional development projects that benefit not only the individuals involved but also the education community and the institution. Professional development activities must be carefully planned, and all stakeholders must be consulted.

- Chapter 9: Grant-making as service
  Grant procurement is often considered a research endeavor, but it does not necessarily have to be, and there are certainly aspects of it that can fall into the service category.

- Chapter 10: Writing references and other service
  The service described in this chapter is not always recognized or rewarded, but it can make a difference for both the person who serves and those who are served.

Conclusion

The *Work of Faculty* report (AAUP, 1994) best sums up the point of and need for service:

Service represents enlightened self-interest on the part of faculty, for whom work on the curriculum, shared governance, academic freedom, and peer review comprise the scholar's and teacher's contributions to the shaping and building of the institution. In addition, it is through service that the professional disciplines communicate and that the exchange of scholarship, by means of conferences and publications, is made feasible. And it is through service that the faculties of our colleges and universities offer their professional knowledge, skills, and advice to their communities. The faculty's commitment to the public welfare, as well as its reinvestment in the health and continuing social and intellectual utility of the academy, is expressed to a considerable extent by what we refer to as service. It is a vital component of our collective lives and of our role in society.

(n.p.)

We hope this text will take some of the mystery that Ward (2010) speaks of out of the service role for faculty, staff, and students and support better understanding of this essential component of education.

Recommended Resources

- Gardner, S., & Mendoza, P. (Eds.). (2010). *On becoming a scholar: Socialization and development in doctoral education.* Sterling, VA: Stylus.

  This text explores issues surrounding doctoral student education in service and other areas and provides insight into graduate student development, epistemologies, and more.

- Kezar, A., Chambers, T., & Burkhardt, J. (2005). *Higher education for the public good: Emerging voices from a national movement.* San Francisco, CA: Jossey-Bass/Wiley.

  This text addresses how collaboration across societal sectors, including higher education, can contribute to society.

Guided Practice

1. Using an Internet search engine, go online and try to find *definitions* of "service" from at least three of the type of education organization you currently or might work for. How do the definitions compare?
2. Search the Web for service *requirements* from three like education organizations (universities, colleges, schools). How do they compare? To what do you attribute the differences?
3. Rank the service types (e.g., presentations, fundraising, reviewing) in this text in order of importance (in your opinion). Discuss your ranking with your peers.

References

American Association of University Professors (AAUP). (1994). *The work of faculty: Expectations, priorities, and rewards.* Retrieved 11 November 2014 from www.aaup.org/report/work-faculty-expectations-priorities-and-rewards

Chambers, T. (2005). The special role of higher education in society: As a public good for the public good. In A. Kezar, T. Chambers, & J. Burkhardt (Eds.), *Higher education for the public good: Emerging voices from a national movement* (Chapter 1, pp. 3–22). San Francisco, CA: Jossey-Bass/Wiley.

Comerford, K. (2014). *Statement of service philosophy.* Retrieved 20 October 2014 from http://sites.google.com/a/georgiasouthern.edu/kcomerfo/service-philosophy

Mendoza, P., & Gardner, S. (2010). The PhD in the United States. In S. Gardner & P. Mendoza (Eds.), *On becoming a scholar: Socialization and development in doctoral education* (pp. 11–26). Sterling, VA: Stylus.

TCU. (2012). *Report on faculty service at TCU.* Retrieved 9 October 2014 from http://www.fsn.tcu.edu/TPG/TP&G%20Report%20on%20Service%20Final.pdf

UC-Berkeley, (2007). *Guidelines for evaluation of service in faculty performance review.* Retrieved 9 October 2014 from http://apo.berkeley.edu/guidelines_for_evaluation_of_service.pdf

UT-Chattanooga. (2013). *Best practices for evaluating faculty service.* Retrieved 9 October 2014 from www.utc.edu/faculty-senate/pdfs/hbappendixservice.pdf

Ward, K. (2003). Faculty service roles and the scholarship of engagement. *ASHE-ERIC Higher Education Report, 29,* 5. San Francisco, CA: Wiley/ Jossey-Bass.

Ward, K. (2010). Doctoral student socialization for service. In S. Gardner & P. Mendoza (Eds.), *On becoming a scholar: Socialization and development in doctoral education* (pp. 57–77). Sterling, VA: Stylus.

2

PRESENTATIONS

Abstract examples for two conference presentations:

As Internet use becomes ever more ubiquitous in language class-rooms worldwide, media literacy does not seem to be increasing at the same pace. From images to sound bites, the Internet is rampant with misinformation, partial information, and seemingly valid infor-mation that needs to be closely assessed by users. Without the knowl-edge and skills to recognize and evaluate bias, however, students could be misled or worse. The presenters will discuss media literacy principles, present six tasks, and ask the audience to participate in a sample media literacy activity. Handouts will be included. 91 words

The Common Core State Standards draw attention to text complexity. As more and more students read graphic novels, understanding a graphic novel's text complexity assumes importance. In addition, since many graphic novels have their roots in a literary version, a question also arises as to whether they hold the same level of complexity as their traditional counterpart. This presentation addresses those questions. 62 words

Overview

In other chapters, we explore written forms of service to the profession. In this chapter, we delve into the contribution and importance of presentations. All presentations are intended to "show, describe, or explain something to a group of people" (Merriam-Webster, n.d.). Shulman (2004) adds that "it's clear that scholarship entails an artifact, a product, some form of community property that can be shared, discussed, critiqued, exchanged, and built upon" (p. 142). Presentations can differ in their specific purposes (e.g., to share personal research, synthesize existing scholarship, guide teachers' classroom practices, propose theoretical ideas, or, as in the examples that start this chapter, a combination of these). Presentations can also address different audiences, ranging from teachers to researchers to policy makers. They can be invited, recommended for acceptance by a committee of reviewers, or result from an invitation by a K–12 school district (the latter is addressed in Chapter 8). Regardless of the specific purpose, audience, or starting point, presentations hold personal and professional value for those in academia. This is in part because engaging in presentations can enhance one's vita (an important concern for promotion and tenure), provide opportunities for collaboration, and contribute to professional growth. While the creation of a presentation might seem straightforward and well understood, creating a proposal that will be accepted for presentation warrants closer attention.

This chapter addresses:

- Exploring the benefits of presenting
- Guidelines for presenting

- Responsibilities of presenters
- The roles of technology in presentations
- Listing presentations on a CV or résumé

Exploring the Benefits of Presenting

Several claims were made above about the benefits of presenting. This section considers the benefits in more depth, including those of attending a forum, such as a conference, for presentation. However, there are also some limitations of presenting, and attending to both positions allows educators to make their own choices about whether and why to present.

First, presentations do have the potential to strengthen a professional profile. Not only do they provide a line on the vita, but they can also support a publication record if the presenter chooses to publish the presentation in a journal or conference proceedings. In addition, the time limit that comes with a presentation forces the presenter to condense information and present potentially complex ideas cogently. This can support clarity if submitted for publication and, combined with the comments from reviewers of the conference proposal and the discussant (if there is one), offer additional review to consider before submission to a journal. Making a commitment to turn presentations into publications can keep the cycle of productivity rolling.

Further, presentations that include a refereed process can contribute to the regard of any presentation, something important for promotion and tenure, as well as add to the prestige that might lead to an invitation to present in the future.

Presentations can also provide opportunities to collaborate. The obvious possibility includes working with others for the presentation—an idea that will be fully addressed in the next section. However, the chance for future collaborative endeavors can also stem from the people you meet at the presentation forum and the interests you share. These networking benefits can lead to rich and enduring collaborative work.

In addition, professional growth can occur as part of creating and sharing a presentation. Questions turn into projects with a specific presentation outlet in mind. Attending the presentations of others can spark new ideas or deepen those already considered.

On the other hand, presentations also come with time and expense; these go beyond the financial and the time spent in preparing and giving the talk. They also take time away—especially from teaching. Some teaching tasks can be accomplished while away, for example grading, responding to students' queries, and planning for the next session. Designating time for those tasks can lessen other benefits from being at a conference (or other presentation forum), as they may take time away from attending other sessions, networking, and interacting with professional friends whom you see too seldom. Further, it might be difficult to compensate for missing classes. While some students might be happy to have a "day off," some students might resent it and indicate their displeasure on the all-important student evaluations. To lessen this possible consequence, presenters can build any absences into the syllabus and note a productive and beneficial alternative for students (e.g., a work period for an upcoming product, a chance for collaboration around a group project).

In the end, the process and products involved in presenting afford the presenter more pluses than minuses. When intentionally selected and professionally created, they can expand the knowledge base for the presenter and inform the wider educational community.

Guidelines for Presenting

Although the idea seems simple enough on the surface, a scholarly presentation includes more than just standing up and speaking.

Presenters must choose the appropriate forum, be accepted to present (in most contexts), create a presentation that will be engaging to the audience, and develop ways to interact with that audience to get the main points across. Guidelines for doing so are outlined in what follows.

Gathering Information

Before you begin to create a presentation, it is helpful to have a good understanding of the forums in which presentations in your area are made. Attending conference presentations, local brown bags, or other opportunities to view professional presentations is a good first step. In addition, applying to review proposals for an organization with which you are associated will also provide information about what others plan to present and how the proposals are evaluated. Working with a more experienced presenter is often a good choice for those new to the venue, as is running your ideas and proposal past a colleague or mentor.

Choosing a Topic, Venue, and Audience

We assume that any sharing of information in a presentation format should come from a place of informed knowledge and personal interest on the presenter's part. However, it's not enough just to know about something; choosing an appropriate topic, venue, and audience are essential for an effective presentation.

The topic obviously assumes foremost importance. For invited talks, sometimes the invitation is issued with a topic already in mind. In other forums, such as large conferences, many topics are of interest to participants; these are typically listed in the call for proposals. Potential presenters should read the call or invitation carefully in order to be sure that the proposed topic fits with the theme. For example, Figure 2.1 lists topics that might be addressed at the National Council for the Teaching of Mathematics conference. Because they are specifically listed, presentations that propose to address one or more of these topics are more likely to get accepted, but that does not mean that other topics will not fit.

Figure 2.1   Conference strands (NCTM, 2015).

Focus Strands

Assessing the Common Core—This strand offers sessions, bursts, and gallery workshops designed for teachers, teacher leaders, and math specialists/coaches to focus on effective and efficient assessment practices. This includes a focus on both formative and summative assessment. In these situations, participants will engage in discussions and reflect on activities that address the role of both formative and summative assessments, consider the resulting data that uncovers student thinking and reasoning, and learn how to identify unfinished learning and strategically move student learning forward.

Integrating Math With Other Disciplines—This strand focuses on the importance of mathematics beyond the classroom. The goal of this strand is to feature the relevance of mathematics for students through the connections in visual, performing and literal arts, the social sciences, as well as STEM–related topics. Sessions might also address the integration of mathematics and Next Generation Science Standards.

Problems Worth Solving—This strand focuses on finding, adapting and/or designing, and implementing worthwhile mathematical tasks. The primary goal for the strand is to develop a deeper understanding about what makes a task worthwhile and consider the influence of these tasks on developing mathematical habits of mind, such as those articulated

Figure 2.1 (Continued)

in the Standards for Mathematical Practice. Throughout the strand, participants should consider the following questions:

1. What makes a problem "worth solving"? What are the potential influences of worthwhile tasks on student thinking and reasoning?
2. What mathematical teaching practices (c.f. Principles to Action) support implementation of worthwhile tasks? What are specific actions and decisions a teacher would make?
3. How might a teacher elicit students' mathematical thinking and orient students toward one another and the discipline? What are the benefits and drawbacks of various approaches?

Supporting Students as Learners—Explorations, professional development concepts, ideas, and suggestions for engaging mathematics teachers who are on the path of lifelong learning is the focus of the Supporting Teachers as Learners Strand. Designed for novice and experienced teachers alike, the strand's sessions will provide an opportunity for participants to discuss and explore programs, products, and processes that will enhance the knowledge and instructional practice of teachers of mathematics.

Supporting Teachers as Learners—This strand is at the heart of what teaching mathematics is all about. This strand presents best ideas, strategies, practices and curricula, and so forth that can be used to support students as learners of mathematics. Participants will go forward from the strand's sessions with a renewed sense of possibilities for empowering all students to actively engage in and ultimately learn mathematics.

Figure 2.1 (Continued)

Conference Strands

In addition to the focus strands listed, don't forget to check out the following conference strand:

New Teacher Strand—This strand offers sessions and gallery workshops targeting the questions and concerns of new teachers and those training to become teachers. Presentations are grade-band specific and include topics from management and motivation to engaging struggling students to a celebration of those entering and just beginning their teaching careers. Learn, network with other new teachers, and get your questions answered. The strand targets early-career teachers and those working on certification; all are welcome.

Annual Meeting Topics

In addition to the focus strands, presentations will cover current math education topics, including the following:

Algebra
Assessment
Calculus & Discrete Mathematics
Data Analysis & Probability
Discourse
Effective Teaching Practices
Equity & Diversity Issues
Geometry & Measurement
Number & Operations
Problem Solving
Professional Development, Coaching, & Mentoring
Reasoning, Sense Making, Proofs
Tasks, Task Development
Technology

For academic presentations, a decision about venue might actually occur first, with the audience dictated by that choice. For example, presenting at the yearly International TESOL conference provides the opportunity to give an academic session, a practical workshop, a poster session, or a full-day preconference institute. The request for proposals also commonly asks presenters to choose the most likely audience for their presentation type and content—from elementary teachers to higher education teacher educators to researchers, from people new to the topic to those more experienced. For example, Appendix 2-A provides a proposal form from the Association for Literacy Educators and Literacy. (The sample proposal forms mentioned in this section also provide important background for the content of the next section.)

Matching the topic, forum, and audience is one requirement reviewers will check for in every proposal. If the topic does not fit the conference theme, the forum is not the right place (too practical or too research based, for example), or the audience does not seem to suit the presentation content, the proposal could be rejected.

Several guidelines can assist with this part of the decision-making process:

1. Consider your interests, context, and experience. For example, Mary's professional interests combine various aspects of literacy with a primary focus on middle-level educators and their students. She also jointly considers herself a teacher educator and researcher, which further directs her decisions about presentations. In addition, she works within a university setting. Based on her interests and with a practical consideration of travel costs and time, Mary's presentation choices should be intentional and strategic. She would not typically, for example, present at a conference meant for preschool science teaching. On the other

hand, conferences such as those put on by the American Education Research Association (AERA), the National Council of Teachers of English (NCTE), and the Literacy Research Council (LRC) address the issues and level that she is interested in on international and national levels. (Those who are less experienced in presenting might want to start at a regional or local level, for example, at conferences or meetings conducted by local affiliates of the larger organization). For other faculty, staff, and students, differences in the contextual variables would necessarily shift the decision making surrounding topics and venue.

2. Be consistent/coherent. Mary regularly presents at the three conferences mentioned, forcing her to have work in place that allows for a strong proposal submission. This regularity also supports a generally agreed-upon promotion and tenure expectation that one's research be ongoing and without gaps. While NCTE and LRC are directly related to her areas of expertise, she selects AERA because of its status across various disciplines and its regard by a broad range of educational stakeholders. It also has a middle-level Special Interest Group that feeds her middle-level interests.

3. Understand your audience. Mary often presents to middle-level teachers, researchers, or teacher educators, but not all in the same venue. She addresses her presentation to a specific audience so the content and topic have value for the participants.

In combination, the array of outlets where Mary presents offers straightforward links to how she defines herself. Their names and her proposal titles indicate coherency. For example, the professional organizations that offer the conferences have literacy in their names (e.g., Association of Literacy Educators and Researchers, National Literacy Association, International Literacy Association) or the age group on which she primarily focuses (i.e., Association of Middle Level Education). The proposal titles include the same links (e.g., *A Middle-Level Exclusive: Empirical Evidence for Middle-Level Literacy Practices, Trends, and Topics: Books for the Literacy Community, The Power of Why in Literacy Learning: Connecting a Literacy Curriculum to Students' Lives*). This need for coherence is a common tenure and promotion expectation Mary can easily explain when she needs to compose a research or teaching statement for promotion or annual review.

A few specific points embedded in the examples lead to several additional general recommendations:

- Before you begin your quest to present, define who you are as a professional, specify the professional identity you want to convey to a wider constituency, and clarify the expectations that accompany your place of employment.
- Remain mindful of the overall contribution of any presentation to your personal goals and professional responsibilities. Ask yourself whether the time and cost justify moving a proposal forward.
- Think topic coherence. Submitting proposals to 16 conferences and having them accepted might be flattering and tempting, but if they do not coalesce around identifiable themes, they might not advantage an upward professional and national trajectory. That is in addition to the immense amount of time and resources preparing for 16 conferences could take! Most higher education institutions require two national presentations per year, and making these presentations worthwhile and talked about might have a greater impact than presenting 16 times.

Writing and Submitting a Proposal

If you hold membership in the organizations you target for presentations, you will automatically receive information about upcoming conferences and links to the proposal submission process (if not, they are typically available on the organization's website). Do not assume, however, that one organization's expectations coincide with another. Proposal pieces vary in length, areas expected for inclusion, and the submission process. Again, one of the most important aspects of getting a proposal accepted is reading and understanding the call for proposals. Additional guidelines in this area include:

- Be prompt. A noted due date is firm. The online site, which most conferences now use, will make late submissions impossible, so note the due date and plan early in case glitches occur. In the proposal form in Appendix 2-B, the due date comes first in the AERA posting and is placed in bold print. The due date holds a prominent placement at the end of the LRA posting in Appendix 2-C. The message is clear: Submit on time.

- Complete the form accurately. Some organizations provide samples of successful submissions. Read them and, instead of just reading for content, also pay close attention to their organizational and format features. Suggestions for obtaining additional information are provided for a reason. Go to them and read them carefully. On the AERA website, for example, the first recommendation is to read the Call for Submissions. Skipping this would omit the opportunity to learn about word length, a requirement to indicate Institutional Review Board (IRB) approval for research involving human subjects, and the limitations for appearing on the program. The LRA explanation also offers more specific guidance by referencing links to appendices and other additional information.

- Be mindful of the type of presentation you select. While paper proposals receive more prime time, a roundtable or poster session provides more opportunity to talk about your work and more interaction with those who attend. Some roundtables and poster sessions are also designed for work in progress, which might better suit the status of your work and offer important guidance for its continuation. Proposals for any format go through a careful review process and get your name on the program, so do not shy away from the presentation format that best suits your work. Other proposal options also exist for some conferences (e.g., alternative formats and panels).

- Address requirements. The AERA program proposal includes six items: (1) objectives; (2) perspectives or theoretical foundations; (3) methods, techniques, or modes of inquiry; (4) data sources; (5) results; and (6) significance. LRA notes topics and their order; it also requires an explanation of the interest for conference attendees. Using section requirements as headings for a proposal will confirm that none were overlooked. Space limitations demand the need to be thorough and succinct without sacrificing the noted expectations.

Figure 2.2 contains an example of a conference proposal for a theoretical presentation. This and the empirical and practical examples in Appendices 2-D and 2-E demonstrate not only the different types of proposals but the different ways in which they can be written.

Figure 2.2 Proposal for a theoretical presentation.

STEM: Where Does Literacy Fit?

Abstract

Within educational reform, STEM takes center stage. The combined attention to the four areas STEM addresses (science, technology, engineering, and math) is seen as the

Figure 2.2 (Continued)

engine that will propel students to a brighter future and secure our nation's global prominence and influence. This leaves many educators to reconsider the role of literacy within this discipline-driven environment. This presentation tackles that issue by reframing STEM and placing literacy at the heart of STEM goals.

Purpose

Several purposes guide this presentation. First, it intends to broaden the definition of STEM by positioning literacy as an integral rather than assumed or tangential component for learning within these four disciplines. To accomplish this intention, it then explores the need for teacher educators to evaluate current content-area reading courses for their responsiveness to STEM literacy learning. Finally, it suggests a two-pronged assessment for STEM that captures teachers' ability to nurture STEM literacy and identifies their students' achievements.

Major Content

Several lines of scholarship inform this presentation. One is the long tradition of research linked to content-area literacy. From this important line of research, teachers learned to test and address prior knowledge, attend to vocabulary, pay close attention to text structure, and consider the composite of attributes that make a text appropriate or ill suited for students (e.g., Lenski & Lewis, 2008). Not all the news identified during this period was good. The educational community also discovered that pre- and in-service teachers resist the concept of content-area literacy and do not willingly embrace their responsibility to attend to its recommendations (O'Brian, Stewart, & Moje, 1995). In addition,

Figure 2.2 (Continued)

Duke (2000) unveiled the scant attention given by teachers of young children to reading the types of text prominent in the disciplines. Other scholars noted the overall gap between reading stories and understanding exposition that exists for older readers (Guthrie & Davis, 2003). Recently, the conversation changed in tone and terms. Now, literacy scholars talk about literacy within the disciplines and consider multiple literacies (e.g., Shanahan, 2004). However, STEM has surpassed an attention to other disciplines and set aside a more direct inclusion of literacy. In this STEM dialogue, literacy receives little direct attention. Instead, science, technology, engineering, and math are noted, and literacy too often remains an unspoken assumption. The natural alliance between any discipline and literacy learning remains, but it is not as directly addressed within STEM as some would hope. Therefore it becomes important to maintain literacy's prominence in these newer discussions while simultaneously defusing the negative aspects that bred contempt toward the infusion of literacy research in decades past. This presentation explores possible tactics: (1) revitalizing content-area literacy courses by renaming them and redirecting their direction, (2) remaining mindful of the unique characteristics of literacy across the disciplines, (3) expecting STEM teachers to maintain an allegiance to their specific discipline, and (4) redirecting STEM from a combination of specific subjects to a broader agenda: sticking to elements that matter—reading and writing as historians, scientists, artists, mathematicians, and scientists.

Methods of Presenting

The presentation will include a slide show and provide participants handouts from it. Throughout the time span for this

Figure 2.2 (Continued)

> presentation, input from those in attendance will be solicited. The intention is that the formal presentation pieces will contribute to a lively exchange with participants. The ultimate hope is that all will leave with a renewed awareness of STEM initiatives and a commitment to have literacy remain a centerpiece of them.

Creating the Presentation and Audience Materials

Once you submit your proposal and it has been accepted, the hard work begins of creating the presentation's content.

- Read the reviewers' comments (if available). Not all organizations provide comments from proposal reviewers, but if they are provided, these comments can direct you to points that need further clarification, minimize a need for deep attention to other points, and provide a sense of the overall impression the reviewers hold.

- Provide the discussant copy. Some conferences expect that if you are presenting a research paper, you will submit it directly to a discussant or an online location several weeks in advance to allow time for the discussant to frame his or her comments; the discussant will provide a public response regarding your work, and you want it to stem from an informed understanding of your ideas. Just like the reviewers' comments can improve the content of a presentation, a discussant's comments can also alert you to places of strength and places that warrant further attention as you move toward publication. Allow the discussant the expected time to do more than peruse your paper and then pay attention to the comments.

- Make the presentation fit the time allotted. Clarify the time you have and hold yourself to it. Most conference attendees can recall more than one session where presenters surpass their allotted time, ignoring the "0 time left" that appears from the person chairing the session or the people arriving for the next session. Whether impacting the time left to people who share a combined paper session or the person next using the room, it creates inconvenience and leaves an impression of disregard for others. Anyone can get caught up in the moment and bring in more ideas than intended; rehearsing your talk and noting the points you want to make can help maintain the intended flow and time frame for the presentation.

- Create a visual. The use of a slide show is an option instead of a requirement. However, most presenters create one, and most audience members expect one. While presenters tend to use Microsoft PowerPoint, other options such as Prezi, Google Present, PowToon, and SlideRocket might better suit you and your content. (Refer to Turnbull, n.d., for a synopsis of these and other web-based alternatives.) Regardless of the platform choice you make, remember that the things you include (from photos to words to video) should enhance the points you want to make rather than provide flashiness that, however memorable, might distract the audience from grasping the heart of your talk. When a slide involves words, a minimalist approach often works best. Experts often recommend no more than six words per slide. The number of slides depends on time and purpose.

The concept of "death by PowerPoint" is defined as the "poor use of presentation software" (Rouse, 2013). The main caution in using a slide show is to be careful of distancing an audience from the points that matter most. McMillan's (2010) YouTube video captures additional hindrances to an informative PowerPoint presentation.

Many other updated and useful resources exist around the Internet that can help with the design of media for presentations.

Considering Formal and Informal Presentation Styles

Not too long ago, professional presentations were accompanied by a general sense of formality. Those stipulations, from acceptable attire to language that promoted the appearance of objectivity (i.e., the avoidance of personal pronouns) have loosened. However, presenters need to understand the norms that guide the venues selected for their work—and these can vary considerably. At many conferences, jeans might be in order on nonpresentation days, but something more in keeping with "business casual" (generally defined for men as a shirt with a collar such as a casual shirt, a polo shirt, or a golf shirt worn with slacks; for women, it means casual skirts, dresses, pants, and blouses) might be more customary on the day of the presentation. Comparable distinctions can arise for presentation styles. At research conferences, the expectation might be for formal adherence to the paper sections noted by APA specifications. As previously mentioned, these conferences might also expect the avoidance of personal pronouns in the presentation of ideas. Others might expect that a presentation of a paper be just that—a reading of the paper with little digression from it. On the other hand, a practical presentation or workshop might involve a lot of informal interactions among presenters and participants. While some of these different possibilities might seem stilted and out of step with the times, a presenter, especially if making a first-time appearance, wants attention to remain on his or her comments. Falling outside the conference norms can introduce a redirection of attention away from the key points of the presentation. In other words, presenters should be aware of the level of formality in both dress and presentation and try to follow it as closely as possible.

Responsibilities of Presenters: Alone or With Collaborators

Some of the responsibilities of presenters can be inferred from previous comments: meeting the dates for submission, honoring time limitations, creating a mindful and informative presentation, creating a slide show that enhances rather than detracts from the big ideas, complying with the expectations set for presenters (e.g., submitting a paper to discussants), and having appropriate and carefully designed handouts. Handouts serve as reminders of what presentation participants heard and viewed. Numerous web-based sites offer suggestions for quality handouts (e.g., Glick, 2010; Mitchell, 2010). These expectations remain whether the presentation is an individual or collaborative enterprise. However, collaboration introduces a few additional items to consider. With a presentation partner, the division of responsibilities during the presentation needs to allow for transitions from speaker to speaker. These should be fluid rather than intrusive and continue to stay within time limitations. Carefully determining transitional comments in advance can contribute to this smooth exchange of presenters. The responsibilities of the presentation proposal and presentation divisions also need to be agreed on and truly collaborative. While one person might take the lead, each person needs to make a unique and important contribution; this might be as simple as clarifying the central ideas to address and distributing them across presenters. The important point is that points are collaboratively identified in advance and presentation materials inspected to make sure they are included. Especially with today's emphasis on large and interdisciplinary projects, numerous collaborators can contribute; therefore, decisions must be made about the number of people who can reasonably participate when the product of the work is a presentation. Finally, the inclusion of a person's name must stem from an ongoing involvement with the project. When well implemented, collaboration can ease the load of the work presentations entail, bring multiple perspectives to bear on the work, and foster an appreciation and understanding of rich collaborations.

The Roles of Technology in Presentations

In addition to the use of a slide show in creating a presentation (as mentioned previously), other technology options also exist—and will continue to expand. Considering them can strengthen the impact of your ideas, increase audience involvement during the presentation, and create opportunities for further involvement with the presentation's ideas. For example, presenters can invite audience members to use their smartphones to text questions to them during their presentation. They then monitor the submitted questions and incorporate them into their final comments and, if time runs out, respond to them afterward. The use of such backfeed (or a "backchannel" provided by platforms such as Twitter) offers a more sophisticated way to encourage response. It also allows an ability to read more comments on a post; see likes and reposts; save comments, likes, and posts; and encourage discussion. A website can also be created for comments and information. Further, sharing e-mail addresses with the audience (usually placed on the initial slide) has become a standard expectation.

Listing Presentations on a CV or Résumé

Since one purpose of making a presentation is to enhance your professional portfolio and let others know of it, including it on a résumé or curriculum vita is important. Following is a list of suggestions from the APA Manual (APA, 2010):

- Put your name at the beginning of the reference, with the last name followed by a comma and then your first initial followed by a period.

- Put the month and year of the presentation in parentheses after the period, with a comma after the month. Put a period outside the parentheses.
- Italicize the title of the presentation. With the exception of proper nouns, only capitalize the first letter of the title and the first letter after a colon.
- Give a one-sentence description of the presentation. Include information about the audience and the location.
- Indent every line except the first line so that your last name is separated from the body of the reference.

Following these recommendations, an APA–style vita entry for a presentation might look like that in Figure 2.3.

Because a vita does not necessarily demand compliance with APA format, organizing the presentations by professional organization and the year might do more to evidence the systematic and coherent attributes of the presentations. If going this route, the citations might take on the format in Figure 2.4.

Entries could also be organized according to year, topic, or type of presentation; presenters should refer to their institutional preferences and, where none exist, to the most logical format for their work.

Figure 2.3 Example APA style for a presentation entry.

Roe, M. (October, 2015). *Literacy: Reading redux or reading gone?* Paper presented at ALER, Cost Mesa, California.

Figure 2.4 Alternate presentation entry.

Name of Organization That Sponsors the Conference
Location of conference
Year of presentation—*Title of Presentation*

Second Organization That Sponsors the Conference
Location of conference
Year of presentation—*Title of Presentation*

Conclusion

A successful presentation submission, then, begins with a good idea, defined here as a topic that resonates with the conference's orientation and mission. Exploring the possibilities of iPads for learning mathematics would perhaps better suit a conference for practitioners, while reporting the effects of virtual manipulatives on reading achievement suggests a research-oriented venue. From the initial selection of a topic and the identification of a venue, the content depends on the guidelines for submissions. Remember, completing each stage of this process with appropriate attention to it contributes to your professional persona.

Regardless of the type of presentation, it can offer personal and professional benefits. The following guidelines, taken from the various sections of this chapter, capture suggestions that promote these possibilities:

1. Carefully consider the interplay among the presentation's topic, the selection of a venue, and the audience.
2. Scour the selected conference's website to understand the requirements for submitting a successful proposal and offering a presentation in alignment with presentation and presenter guidelines and expectations.

3. If using a slide show, remain focused on the ideas you want to convey and use presentation tools in service of them.
4. Maintain an ability to explain the links between a presentation and your professional goals and roles.

Recommended Resources

- Berk, R. A. (2003). *Professors are from Mars, students are from Snickers: How to write and deliver humor in the classroom and in professional presentations.* Sterling, VA: Stylus Publishing, LLC.

  These ideas are suited for more information presentations or for adding a lighthearted touch to more formal designs.

- Fenrich, P. (1998). *Practical guidelines for creating instructional multimedia applications.* Hinsdale, IL: Dryden Press.

  Especially helpful when considering more than text in a PowerPoint presentation.

- Hess, G. R., Tosney, K. W., & Liegel, L. H. (2009). Creating effective poster presentations: AMEE Guide no. 40*. *Medical Teacher, 31*(4), 319–321.

  This resource extends to poster presentations—a format with increased popularity, but not addressed in this chapter. While focused on the medical community, its suggestions are applicable beyond that field.

- Platow, M. (2002). *Giving professional presentations in the behavioral sciences and related fields: A practical guide for the novice, the nervous, and the nonchalant.* Florence, KY: Psychology Press.

  This text expands on the ideas noted in this chapter.

Guided Practice

1. Decide on three professional organizations you might consider for presentations. Then visit their websites to find information about their conferences. Insert due dates for submitting a proposal into your calendar. Then note their submission and presentation processes so you are prepared for them when and if you decide to submit.

2. Consider your interests and context and create a proposal for an organization for review by peers or colleagues. Include the abstract and conference book statements.

3. If you have previously presented, consult your vita to see if your presentations are cited to follow APA or other options. If you used another option, make sure you are consistent and that your choices highlight your interests and goals. If you have never written vita citations previously, decide which option you intend to use and write sample citations that follow your choice.

4. Consult your promotion and tenure guidelines (or those for a university where you would like to work) to understand the role of presentations in promotion and tenure.

References

American Psychological Association (APA). (2009). *Publication manual of the American Psychological Association.* Washington, DC: APA.

Glick, F. (2010). *Presentation design and delivery handout.* Accessed 22 August 2015 from http://web.stanford.edu/group/eweek/2010/media/ Presentation_Design_handout.pdf.

McMillan, D. (2010). *Life after death by PowerPoint.* Retrieved 20 August 2015 from https://www.youtube.com/user/donmcmillancomedy.

Merriam Webster (n.d.). *Presentation.* Retrieved 22 August 2015 from www. merriam-webster.com/dictionary/presentation.

Mitchell, O. (2010). *13 best practice tips for effective handouts.* Retrieved 20 August 2015 from www.speakingaboutpresenting.com/delivery/ presentation-handouts/.

NCTM. (2015). *Program and presentations.* Retrieved 22 August 2015 from www.nctm.org/Conferences-and-Professional-Development/Annual-Meeting-and-Exposition/Program-and-Presentations/.

Rouse, M. (2013, August). *Death by PowerPoint.* WhatIs.com. Retrieved 22 August 2015 from http://whatis.techtarget.com/definition/death-by-PowerPoint.

Shulman, L. S. (2004). *Teaching as community property: Essays on higher education.* San Francisco, CA: Wiley.

Turnbull, C. (n.d.). *6 web-based alternatives to Microsoft PowerPoint.* Retrieved 22 August 2015 from http://workawesome.com/software/6-web-based-alternatives-to-microsoft-powerpoint/.

**Proposal Example From the Association for
Literacy Educators and Researchers**

ALER Conference
Conference Theme: The Joy of Teaching Literacy

Program Proposal

I. Title of Presentation
    (Type the title as you wish it to appear in the conference
    program if the proposal is accepted.)
II. Type of Presentation (Check one)
    ___ Symposium (80 minutes)
    ___ Roundtable (25 minutes)
    ___ Session (25 minutes)
    ___ Workshop (50 minutes)
    ___ Workshop (80 minutes)
III. Major Interest Group
    ___ Clinical Reading
    ___ College Reading

____ Adult Learning
____ Teacher Education (includes elementary, middle school, and secondary reading)

IV. The proposal description should include the following sections and be no longer than two single-spaced pages, 12-point font.

   A. *Abstract* (Type the abstract the way you wish it to appear in the program if the proposal is accepted. Abstract should be clear, accurate, and descriptive. Limit 75 words.)

   B. *Purpose(s) or Objective(s)* of the Presentation

   C. *Major Content*

   D. *Methods of Presenting Content* (Overhead projector and screen provided). Individuals who need any other equipment must arrange to rent, bring, or order it from a local supplier at the presenter's own expense.

   E. *Other Important Information* (optional)

No presenter names or institutional affiliations should be included in the proposal.

References and citations strengthen a proposal. Use current APA style.

Submit proposals, along with Presenter Information Forms for each presenter, via e-mail by February 15 to *alerconf2011@uta. edu.*

Deadline for Paper and Session Submissions is July 22

A downloadable Call for Submissions will be available soon. Please review the Call for Submissions, as it contains important information about this year's Annual Meeting theme and submission requirements.

How to Submit

Please review the Call for Submissions (PDF)

Log in

Click "My AERA" at the top of the page

Scroll down to the Annual Meeting and click "Online program portal." Please pay special attention to the six elements that must be addressed in the narrative paper submissions even if the results, conclusions, or findings are not complete or final at the time of the submission. Also, please indicate your preferred type of session and willingness to present in alternative formats at the time of submission.

Appendix 2-C
LRA Call for Proposals

Proposals that are incomplete and/or do not conform to the following guidelines might be rejected without review.

Proposal

A proposal with an accompanying reference list must be submitted as a single PDF or WORD file. The proposal, excluding the reference list and tables or figures, must be **no more than 1500 words**. No more than five (5) tables or figures may be included in the proposal. The proposal should not contain any obvious clues that identify the author(s) of the proposal. (Note: citations of an author's work are permissible if they do not clearly identify the author—APA provides guidelines.) The proposal must present specific information based on the type of session being submitted and detailed as follows:

Paper or Roundtable Sessions

The proposal should address the following in the order specified and as applicable:

(a) purpose; (b) perspective(s) or theoretical framework; (c) methods and/or techniques; (d) data source(s); (e) results, conclusions, and/or interpretations; (f) educational and/or scientific importance of the study; and (g) interest/connection to the audience. Submitters are also encouraged to address the conference theme in one or more of the previous sections (see General Criteria in Section VIII).

Symposia or Alternative Format Sessions

The proposal might be in one of the following two forms:

- A unified summary of all the papers or presentations that addresses the information requested in the preceding instructions for "Paper or Roundtable Sessions"; OR
- An overview of the session followed by summaries of each individual presentation containing the information requested in the preceding instructions for "Paper or Roundtable Sessions." Submitters are also encouraged to address the conference theme in one or more of the previous sections (see General Criteria in Section VIII).

Study Groups

The proposal should address the following in the order specified and as applicable:

(a) importance of the topic; (b) issues to be considered; (c) evidence of members' interest in this area; (d) rationale grounded in current professional literature, including references; (e) an agenda, structure, and organization for the sessions; (f) activities undertaken prior to the meeting to ensure adequate attendance and a successful study group experience; (g) the history and productivity of the group if this is a long-standing study group; and (h) leaders' expertise and experience with the proposed topic. Submitters are also encouraged to address the conference theme in one or more of the previous sections (see General Criteria in Section VIII).

Submission Deadline

Proposals must be submitted electronically **no later than 11:59 PM EST March 4**. Any proposal received after that deadline will not be reviewed.

Sample Empirical Presentation Proposal

The Ways Teachers Do the Things They Do: Differentiation in Middle-Level Literacy Classrooms

Purpose

Differentiation. Teacher educators call for it and researchers explore it. I want to understand its interpretation and use by classroom teachers. In that quest, I am reminded of the words of Clifford Geertz, who states, "If you want to understand what a science is you should look in the first instance not at its theories or its findings, and certainly not what its apologists say about it; you should look at what the practitioners of it do." I act on that suggestion by turning an eye to the differentiation practices of middle school teachers in urban, rural, and suburban settings. This overall goal led to the following specific purposes: (1) to identify teachers' understandings of differentiation, (2) to understand their implementation of differentiated instruction for their students, especially those who underachieve or those for whom English is their second language, across an academic year, and (3) to understand students' and teachers' views of the challenges and successes of differentiation attempts.

Theoretical Framework

To consider the complexity of differentiation, I drew upon several lines of inquiry. I initially sought to unveil how scholars use this term. Several definitions arose. In the first, scholars like Turner (2005) and Jimenez (1997) address differences within an identified group of students or specify a component of literacy and offered various strategies for addressing it. They do not directly use the term *differentiation* but do promote the importance of instructional options. In a second direction, scholars pose suggestions of things that teachers might do and offer directions for teachers to follow (e.g., Gregory & Chapman, 2007). Others, like Tomlinson (2001), treat differentiation as a process. Using this definition, they encourage teachers to consider categories such as content, process, and product. Others hitch differentiation to assessment and underscore a movement from assessment to lesson design (e.g., Walpole & McKenna, 2007). In general, these scholars treat differentiation as a philosophy—a way of thinking about literacy teaching and learning. A final group proposes technology as a vehicle to enact differentiation. Egbert (2007) offers one example of this group. She explores multimodal presentations and programs such as Thinking Reader and netTrekker as resources for differentiation. I expand beyond these definitions to embrace a more cultural consideration of differentiation. This broader view permits me to go beyond a teacher's classroom walls to consider outside influences that might influence their differentiation beliefs and choices. This review also identified an absence of an attention to differentiation as understood and implemented by classroom teachers. A second theoretical position that informs this work, principled eclecticism, allows the joining of cognitive flexibility (Spiro, Feltovich, & Coulson, 1992) with a view that classroom life is a cultural practice (e.g., Roe & Kleinsasser, 2000). Finally, the robust body of research that seeks to understand quality literacy practices and the environments that promote middle-level students' literacy achievements hold sway (e.g., Deshler, Palincsar, Biancarosa, & Nair, 2007; Pressley, Billman, Perry, Reffit, & Reynolds, 2007). In combination, linking these lines of inquiry holds promise for guiding my quest to understand the multifaceted dimensions a consideration of differentiation for middle-level teachers and students entails.

Research Method

A qualitative design (e.g., Denzin & Lincoln, 2005) matches the direction of my research questions. To expand the breadth of understandings, the research locales included the classrooms of nine teachers at four middle schools in the Northwest. The schools differed by location (one urban, two suburban, and one rural), size, academic organization (integrated language arts and social studies or separate subjects), and student populations (second-language learners, a high incidence of free and reduced lunch, ethnic and cultural diversity).

Data came from several sources: field notes from 135 classroom observations (five observations for each teacher at the onset, middle, and end of the school year), informal conversations with teachers and students, transcribed interviews with the nine teachers and a randomly selected subset of their students, and document analysis. Across the three rounds of observations, I made no attempt to shape the teachers' instructional plans or intervene in their students' daily classroom lives.

Data analysis coincided with processes typical of qualitative method (e.g., Strauss & Corbin, 1990). I began with the field notes for each teacher. I started with each teacher's class-room observations. Initially, I determined an activity episode (Gee, Michaels, & O'Connor, 1992) and noted the planned or in-the-moment modifications the teachers made to accommo-date student differences for each classroom observation. I then collapsed these findings within an observational segment and across the 15 observations. Next, I combined the data across teachers and observational periods. As appropriate, I used fre-quency counts to better understand these teachers' individual strategies and those they shared in common at different points and across a school year. To ensure the accuracy and sufficiency of the labels for each differentiation strategy, I narrowed or expanded the codings to allow representative and finely tuned categories. To analyze the interviews, I expanded upon the classroom codes to label references to differentiation practices. Again, I analyzed individual interviews for the teachers and students and then looked across them. I subjected the various documents to analysis by linking them to the witnessed differ-entiation activities and the teachers' and students' references to them. This intermingling of these data sources (Fielding & Fielding, 1986) allowed a rich understanding of the features of differentiation for these teachers, the forms it took at three points and across a school year, and its attributes within and across various locations and organizational arrangements. It also informed the meaning of differentiation for these teachers and their students (Diesing, 1971). Finally, I returned to existing research to fit these findings within it. The use of Ethnograph, a computer program for analyzing qualitative data, facilitated this emic analysis scheme.

Results

These findings include richly substantiated big pieces and those more nuanced. Here, I straightforwardly offer a sampling of central and uncontested understandings. First, these teachers' attention to differentiation regularly included an affective aspect. This broadens the primarily psychological tone more apparent in existing scholarship about differentiation while contributing to Britzman's (2006) exploration of the emotional component of learning. However, while examples exist for the convergence of affective and psychological pieces for middle-level students' literacy (e.g., Roe, 2001), these teachers seldom united their desire to know their students with academic intentions. Some did use these understandings as a rationale for making exceptions to academic or behavioral expectations. All invoked students' backgrounds to further explain achievement concerns. Second, conformance to a classroom's behavior expectations competed with the teachers' literacy goals. Too often, these teachers settled for behavioral compliance devoid of students' intellectual engagement (Sizer, 1992). While students generally appeared to meet behavior expectations, they struggled to simultaneously acknowledge their social needs and complete classroom activities. Third, classroom activities became the engine that drove teachers' differentiation efforts and students' attention. To support their completion, teachers monitored students' work progression by roaming the room and varying the time spent with individual students. When they paused, they would sit by students to explain or assist their efforts. At other times they directed students to text pages or resources that could provide answers. From their observations and individual interactions, teachers often returned to a whole-class explanation of the task, rephrasing an explanation or modeling a specific process. The intention was very direct: assignment completion. While their instructional comments during the students' completion of assigned tasks often linked to important literacy understandings, they lacked the identification of an audience and the structural features that would increase their power and applicability. Linked to this finding, teachers' attention to a finished product overshadowed their attention to literacy processes. These teachers valued literacy processes, but when they did explain or model a process, it was primarily reactive rather than proactive, offered whole class, and not prompted by formative assessment results. In addition, teachers attended to students' developing a work ethic, and they differentiated to promote it. For example, their activity design often offered choices and fostered students' independence as workers. The teachers further relied on routines to encourage students' development of these dispositions. Finally, these teachers regularly designed classroom activities to replicate the state-mandated tests. They often referenced the students' need to do well on them as justification for these exercises. None of these activities were modified or adjusted to meet student differences and needs.

While these general similarities appeared across teachers, stark differences emerged across their teaching contexts. Teachers at the urban school had more curricular mandates, team meetings, and professional development sessions during the school day. They also had more external supports such as a literacy coach and paraprofessionals. The rural and suburban teachers more often noted the disappearance of support systems (e.g., special programs, personnel, classroom materials). The urban teachers also had more required formative assessments. They received this information in team meetings and discussed what they noted. However, these findings did not seem to inform their daily decisions. For those, they returned to local and external curriculum and testing mandates. The suburban and rural schools acquired data from students' use of a computer testing system where students took multiple-choice tests based on a self-chosen book. The suburban schools identified library books by level that coincided with students' identified reading levels. However, only one suburban teacher expected students to choose a book that coincided with them. At no time during these observations did any teachers create instructional groups based on academic differences or needs identified by the data available to them. All schools did use test results to assign poor-performing students to an additional reading class. Overall, these teacher and context results exposed dimensions of teachers' literacy differentiation beyond the primarily cognitive aspects so prevalent in existing research, questioned the appropriateness of a tendency to focus on teachers' classrooms without simultaneously addressing their teaching context, underscored the importance of strengthening an attention to literacy processes, and confirmed an ongoing need for teachers to link assessment findings, affective concerns, and instructional choices.

Educational Importance

Many teacher educators and researchers propose empirically grounded suggestions for teachers' differentiation of classroom practices. This study's attention to actual classroom practices holds the potential to inform the sufficiency of these existing proposals, identify gaps, and further connect research and practice around the important concept of differentiation. A variety of NRC members, including the teachers and administrators whose numbers are growing, would find this topic and its findings timely and important.

Engagement in Minecraft

Abstract

Teaching is about engaging students, and opportunities for creative language use and social interaction supported by technology can engage learners of all ages. During this half-hour demonstration, participants will be exposed to some of the many engaging tasks that both teachers and language students can perform in the versatile Minecraft environment. Examples from classrooms will be presented, and a variety of resources will be explored.

Description

For its versatility and opportunities for creative language use and social interaction, Minecraft is one of the best deals on the commercial software market. However, the Minecraft environment has not been explored in much depth by language teachers, and little can be found about its uses in both teacher education and language classrooms. This brief multimedia demonstration will start to close that gap by introducing aspects of the Minecraft environment to teachers and teacher educators and providing them with enough information to get started on their own crafting. After providing a quick overview of task engagement, the presenters will interact with the session participants in a walk-through of tasks our students have created and/or performed. Additional tasks will be explained, and questions/comments will be entertained throughout the session.

3

REVIEWING MANUSCRIPTS

Excerpt from a manuscript review:

> I think that the bones of a decent paper are here, but they are not well developed. For example, there is no theoretical framework and no research questions. APA is not always correct and there are a great many comma and apostrophe errors, in addition to wording issues, fragments, and other surface errors. There are many other clarification problems, too. I recommend that the author(s) looks at other research articles for format and content. Specific comments that the author(s) might consider are noted below.

Overview

An important option for service stems from a willingness to review manuscripts submitted for publication and being invited to do so. Peer review is the process by which an author's peers who are recognized researchers in the field read, comment on, and evaluate a manuscript submitted for publication and recommend whether the paper should be published, revised, or rejected. As in the opening excerpt, reviewers need to be able to discern the areas of strength and weakness in a manuscript and be willing to take the time to support the author(s) by describing how the paper might be made publishable. In this chapter, we provide guidance for the process of conducting reviews of manuscripts submitted to peer-reviewed journals. Interestingly, while it is expected as part of the process of publishing in any respected journal, the educational community provides little guidance about *how* to write a review. Individual professional organizations typically provide criteria for areas to address, the appropriate tone to adopt, and some reminders around professional courtesy. The publisher might also arrange a meeting for the editors and members of the editorial board to provide information about the health of the publication and hopes for it. These meetings, too, typically provide little direction regarding the specifics of crafting a review. As Provenzale and Stanley (2006) note, "The process of properly reviewing a manuscript is not intuitive but instead requires training and experience, which are not easily acquired" (p. 848). This chapter combines the general process of getting started with manuscript review with specific recommendations for crafting a well-received review.

This chapter addresses

- Applying to join an editorial review board
- Benefits of reviewing
- Understanding responsibilities of reviewers
- Guidelines for completing reviews
- The roles of technology in reviewing
- Listing reviewing on a CV or résumé

Applying to Join an Editorial Review Board

Selecting any service opportunity deserves a joint consideration of a person's role, interests, and responsibilities. Joining an editorial review board (becoming a journal manuscript reviewer/ referee) is no exception. Most tenure-track academic positions and many graduate programs expect service to the profession, and membership on an editorial review board is one way to meet this expectation. If those features apply to your professional setting, then you are left to examine your interests. The big question to answer is this: Do you enjoy providing feedback to authors regarding their manuscripts? If so, then engaging in this service opportunity can bring you a sense of accomplishment, provide benefit to other authors and the field, and further your involvement with tasks expected of you in regard to service to the profession.

Sometimes joining an editorial board stems from simply volunteering or from being invited by the journal editor. In other cases, you need to apply and receive an invitation. Some application processes are posted to a journal's website. The following example offers a very straightforward directive:

> If you are interested in becoming a reviewer, please send a vita to one of the editors listed above.
>
> (*Literacy Research and Instruction*, www.aleronline.org/?page=lri)

Other journal editors, like the editors of *Journal of Literacy Research*, advertise an open call for self-nominations when the need for additional reviewers arises. Editors then make selections from the received applications. If you are unable to find specific information for a journal of interest, you can contact the current editors for guidance. Remember that this is a selection process, and the acceptability of a request to serve for one journal might not transfer to another.

When selecting a journal to serve, potential reviewers should carefully read the explanation regarding anonymity. Most journal editorial boards are bound by double anonymity (the reviewer does not know the author(s) and the author(s) do not know the reviewer). Some have the authors remain unknown but leave it to the reviewer whether to reveal him or herself. Still others, like the American Mathematical Society, state something like this: "The AMS has a single blind peer-review process in which the reviewers know who the authors of the manuscript are, but the authors do not have access to the information on who the peer reviewers are" (www.ams.org/journals). Each option comes with assurances and possible concerns. Only apply to those whose policy resonates with your professional and personal preferences.

Several things can be done to strengthen a request to serve on an editorial review board. First, carefully analyze the description that accompanies a journal. Look for a fit between its publication orientation and your interests and accomplishments. Those who review your application to review will look for matches between what you do and what they publish. Note the following three journal descriptions as examples:

The *Journal of Teacher Education* (*JTE*) is leading teacher education through the 21st century with timely topics such as field experiences and teacher education; cognitive science and critical thinking; preparing teachers for urban schools; teachers' beliefs; accreditation and certification; selection, retention, and recruitment of minority teachers and teacher leadership; perspectives on leadership; professional ethics in teacher education; and restructuring teacher education.

The *Reading Teacher* is a peer-reviewed journal that provides research-based teaching ideas to literacy educators working with children up to age 12. RT's articles cover topics such as applying research to classroom practice and using strategies to help all learners succeed.

> Reading Research Quarterly (RRQ) welcomes submission of research-oriented manuscripts that make significant contributions to advancing knowledge and understanding of reading and of literacy, broadly defined. Articles published in RRQ are primarily reports of original, rigorously conducted research employing diverse epistemologies, methodologies, methods, and disciplinary perspectives. Other appropriate research-oriented articles include essays concerning new theoretical or methodological perspectives, comprehensive syntheses of research toward developing new understandings, and scholarly analyses of trends and issues in the field. Pilot studies, and other research efforts of limited scope or duration, are not typically considered for publication.

These examples show differences in the journals' orientations; the *Journal of Teacher Education* focuses on teacher education, while *The Reading Teacher* addresses literacy. *Reading Research Quarterly* expects high-quality research, while the *Reading Teacher* holds an orientation toward practitioner-oriented manuscripts, and the *Journal of Teacher Education* lists topics with no specification about format. Your publication record should cohere with the topics as well as the format that describes the thrust of the journal. Simply stated, carefully screen yourself; applying to review for a journal that is a good fit likely saves valuable time for the editors and prevents the disappointment from receiving a rejection letter that you might have avoided.

In addition, to become competitive and improve your chance of selection for more highly ranked journals, reviewers should establish a track record of successful reviewing. For some reviewers, their process began as doctoral students with serving on the review boards for internal publications such as the *Western Journal of Black Studies* housed at Washington State University or *READ: An Online Journal for Literacy Educators* published by the College of Education at Sam Houston State University. From there, a progression to reviewing proposals submitted to conferences sponsored by major professional organizations linked to professional interests further adds to a reviewer's experience. These beginnings can serve to build the experiences that support application for editorial board selection for major journals. Should this steady path continue, vying for an editorship can be a next step. Editors, unlike members of an editorial board, have the final authority about the disposition of a manuscript. The editor of a journal receives the manuscripts with comments back from the expert reviewer(s) and forwards them to the author with a summary recommendation to accept the manuscript and move to publication, revise (with directions for necessary changes), or reject. An editor, or in many cases an editorial team, also holds responsibility for maintaining an effective editorial review board and meeting the managerial requirements that often include working with a publisher such as Sage or Taylor and Francis.

Benefits of Reviewing

As stressed in other chapters, service opportunities come with benefits for the person and the field. Professional organizations could not bring their journals to press without the input of their editors and editorial board members. This free-of-charge service by reviewers holds immense importance, in part because the reviewer always learns something from the manuscripts reviewed and from the practice of reviewing. For example, reviewing brings personal benefits like the chance to preview the latest ideas of colleagues, hone an ability to comment, better understand how to perceive strengths and needs of a manuscript, and, as noted, improve your quality of writing, because reviewers see many strong examples from authors who know how to turn a phrase, exude voice without losing a professional stance, and superbly use headings to guide a reader through a manuscript. Reviewers also experience the challenges that ambiguity and a troubled organization can introduce for a reader and how they diminish otherwise strong ideas. Reviewers can look at these learning opportunities as examples to replicate in their writing or as cautionary notes about things to reconsider and even avoid.

Understanding Responsibilities of Reviewers

Once an applicant has accepted an invitation to serve on an editorial board, the next step is to ferret out the responsibilities the journal expects of reviewers. Each journal comes with an explanation of its expectations for reviewers. These can be found on the journal's website or, in some cases, as a reminder when you receive a request to review. The example review guidelines in Figures 3.1, 3.2, and 3.3 provide an idea of the expectations held for reviewers and thereby offer an opportunity to understand whether the tasks coincide with your expectations, interests, and background.

Figure 3.1 Review guidelines from *RRQ*.

Reading Research Quarterly (*RRQ*; http://onlinelibrary.wiley.com/journal/10.1002/(ISSN)1936-2722)

Guidelines

At its core, research involves making an argument. Researchers make knowledge claims on the basis of theory and evidence linked through a clear chain of reasoning that constitutes the warrant for those claims. The arguments are principled, in that the researcher follows a systematic line of inquiry that is accessible to the scrutiny of others in the research community. The logic of inquiry should also adhere, broadly speaking, to the rules of evidence particular to the disciplinary perspectives (e.g., psychology,

Figure 3.1 (Continued)

sociology, anthropology) being brought to bear on the research question(s).

With this view of research in mind, please consider the following questions as you review a manuscript:

- How have the authors located their inquiry against a background of extant knowledge and assumptions?

- How well have they made connections to relevant research?

- How good is the fit between research question(s) and methodology?

- Have the authors conducted the data collection and analysis appropriately? How strong is the warrant for authors' claims? Is there a clear, coherent chain of reasoning by which the author(s) reached their conclusion(s)? Do you find the authors' argument convincing? Have the authors sufficiently considered alternative explanations and perspectives? Have the authors been open-minded and thorough?
  So what? How is the research significant for informing and improving theory and/or practice?

Some of these questions are more appropriate than others, depending on the nature of the inquiry. Nevertheless, in the final analysis, a piece of research is only as good as the quality of the chain of reasoning by which the researchers organize the extant knowledge and assumptions, their observations and analyses, and their knowledge claims "to create a cogent, persuasive argument" (Shulman, 1997, p. 26).

Figure 3.2 Review guidelines from *JRME*.
Journal for Research in Mathematics Education (JRME;
http://jrme.msubmit.net/)

Reviewers are asked to evaluate the merits of the manuscript and the research described therein. *JRME* does not have a fixed set of criteria to be used by reviewers; however, below are some questions that might be helpful in preparing your review. If you prefer to work offline, you might print the manuscript, draft your review remarks using a word processing program, and cut/paste the text into the blinded review text area.

Research Report

Does the research extend or deepen our understanding of important issues in mathematics education? Does it have the potential to lead the field in new directions?

Do the research questions pertain to issues of significant theoretical or pragmatic concern? Are they well grounded in theory or in prior research?

Is there an appropriate match between the research question(s) and the methods and analyses employed to answer the question(s)?

Does the conduct of the study include the effective application of appropriate data collection, analysis, and interpretation techniques?

Are the claims and conclusions in the manuscript justified in some acceptable way, and do they logically follow from the data or information presented?

Is the writing lucid, clear, and well organized?

Research Commentary

Does the manuscript raise an issue about the nature of the research process?

Figure 3.2 (Continued)

> Does the manuscript analyze the connections between research, policy, and practice?
>
> Does the manuscript analyze trends in policies for funding research?
>
> Does the manuscript stimulate discussion among scholars holding contrasting views about research-related issues?

Note that as research journals, *RRQ* and *JRME* have similar guidelines for their reviewers. This is often but not always the case, so reviewers must read the guidelines carefully. The guidelines from *The Reading Teacher*, in Figure 3.3, focus more on what the reviewer should do than on what the manuscript does.

Figure 3.3 Manuscript review guidelines from *The Reading Teacher*.

> **The Reading Teacher** (http://onlinelibrary.wiley.com/)
>
> **Be constructive.** Reviews should be professional and courteous. Authors invest a great deal in their manuscripts, and your comments to them should be helpful and instructive. If you recommend rejection, provide feedback for improvement or for future studies or articles. You might also suggest other publication outlets.
>
> **Be scholarly.** Substantiate your judgments; don't simply offer opinions. Focus on content, style, reasoning, and audience appropriateness. Is the manuscript original? Does it provide a fresh view or synthesis of existing knowledge? Does it convey the intended message clearly and concisely? Is the literature review adequate? Provide citations when you refer to published sources.

Figure 3.3 (Continued)

Be a reviewer, not a copy editor. Focus on the big issues. Rather than pointing out every flaw, detail only those that most support your recommendation of revision or rejection. However, if the form is so poor that revision would require starting over, rejection is justifiable. Do not spend time noting errors in spelling, punctuation, and grammar. Editorial staff will handle these details.

Be specific. Comments should inform authors and editors of the rationale for your recommendation. Provide authors with substantive, concrete suggestions about the strengths and weaknesses of their work. Regardless of your recommendation, offer extensive comments so that the editors can fairly adjudicate a manuscript in the event of conflicting reviews.

Be open-minded. You might be asked to review a manuscript that employs a theoretical or methodological orientation or cultural perspective different from your own. Evaluate it on its own terms, but don't hesitate to indicate how it might benefit from your perspective.

Be ethical. Our review standard is "double blind": Neither authors nor reviewers are revealed to one another. If you discern an author's identity, the integrity of the review process might be compromised. Please inform journals staff about the conflict of interest.

Manuscripts under review are confidential. Do not discuss, circulate, or quote from manuscripts except in communication with the editors or journals staff. If you are concerned that the material under review has been previously published, alert journals staff.

Be mindful of length. Full-length manuscripts should not exceed 6,000 words (appx. 20 pages). Teaching Tips pieces

Figure 3.3 (Continued)

are typically 1,500 words and focus on a single research-based classroom strategy. Note if the manuscript includes material not essential to its purpose. If you recommend revisions that will extend the text, point the author to nonessential sections that could be deleted or condensed.

Be timely. Always complete your evaluation by the date indicated. If you are unable to do so, contact journals staff immediately.

Be available. Editorial Review Board members review once or twice per month; ad hoc members review as needed, up to 4 or 5 times per year. RT receives over 400 manuscripts annually. Each article is considered by two Editorial Review Board members and one ad hoc reviewer; Teaching Tips are considered by two board members. Appointment to the Editorial Review Board is for the calendar year, and precedes the volume year (September to May) in which members are listed in the journal. Ad hoc reviewers are acknowledged in the final issue of each volume.

Be wired. High-speed Internet connection, e-mail, and up-to-date browser software are required as manuscript review is conducted online. Be in touch. Please inform journals staff of changes in affiliation or extended absences. Keep your contact information current by updating your reviewer profile in the online system. Contact staff any time with questions or concerns. We value your feedback!

As the examples indicate, reviewing guidelines range from more extensively documented expectations to general categories of areas for comment. Note that the differences between a research-oriented outlet such as *RRQ* and one with a practitioner orientation (e.g., *The Reading Teacher*) primarily stem from the distinction between research manuscripts and those that are not. If a word count for the review is not specified, judge the appropriate length of a response by the sufficiency of the comments rather than the number of words used. As Lee (1995) reminds us, "Following any set of guidelines for how to do a review might be helpful, but should not dissuade the creative and caring reviewer from innovating additional reviewing methods" (p. 92). Remember that the overall goal of the collection of comments is to provide an editor with clear direction and support for the final dispensation of the manuscript.

Guidelines for Completing Reviews

Although reviewers might go about their task in different ways, there are general guidelines that help lead to effective reviews. Many of these are provided in Figure 3.3. Additional guidelines include:

Read. Two tasks are indicated by this guideline; first, to read the journal's review guidelines, as noted previously, and second, to read the manuscript being reviewed. This might seem inherent, but instances exist in which the author has read the review comments and then questioned whether the reviewer actually read the manuscript. Commenting that the manuscript needs a limitations section when it already has one not only loses credibility for the reviewer but also does so more publicly for the editor and the journal. Reading the manuscript once to gain the essence of it and then a second time to comment is a highly recommended practice.

Be thorough. Figure 3.4 provides a review form for a refereed journal. Similar to some journals, it has both a rubric and a comments section for reviewers to complete. Ignoring one of these sections means the review is incomplete and does not provide the editor with all the necessary information to make a decision on publication. In addition, a reviewer who has completed only part of the review has not met the responsibilities of the position, including providing suggestions for the author to follow during revision. **Be clear.** For review forms like the one in Figure 3.4, if the details in the comment section do not support the ratings given in the rubric, the editor might ask for additional evidence or ignore the review. Similarly, if the detailed comments cannot be understood because of style or use of overly academic prose, the review is not effective (and is probably a waste of time). Simple and clear comments can provide the best information for all stakeholders.

Figure 3.4 Refereed journal form.

This form should be completed and submitted electronically. Please complete both Parts A and B of the review form before returning to the co-editors at: <**editor@journal.org**>

Part A: Assessment

Please indicate your evaluation of each criterion by placing an "X" in the appropriate column below.

Criteria	Acceptable Without change	Revision needed	Not acceptable	Not applicable
1. Complete and well-organized paper				
2. Significance of the research problem/area				
3. Strength of a conceptual/ theoretical framework				

Figure 3.4 (Continued)

Criteria	Acceptable Without change	Revi-sion needed	Not accept-able	Not applicable
4. Demonstration of a relationship with relevant literature				
5. Clear overview of research design and method				
6. Sound argument and analysis				
7. Implications for research and/or practice				
8. Clarity of expression and accuracy				
9. Adherence to the APA style				

Part B: Recommendation

Please indicate your recommendation based on your assessment in Part A.

Accept as is ( )

Accept pending minor changes ( )

Accept pending major changes ( )

Reject (X)

Figure 3.4 (Continued)

Overall comments/Suggestions for improvement
Please provide detailed comments here.

Be professional. Reviewers should focus on providing comments that are straightforward while being kind and coherent and remain on balance. Focusing on the review purpose and maintaining a helpful and diplomatic stance can soften what might be a blow for the author and provide encouragement to continue in the publication process. Starting a review with a comment about one or more of the manuscript's strengths can help the author understand what not to change, and additional comments can explain what the author might revise.

Keep learning. Reviewing can take time and commitment, and doing it well requires that reviewers be open to learning more about the process. Figure 3.5 presents excerpts from a letter like one an author might receive, a version of which is often also sent to reviewers; it includes the reviews that the editors combined to arrive at a decision. Reading this culminating response provides an important opportunity for reviewers to check their responses to a manuscript with those of other reviewers and the editors. If used wisely, the lessons learned can improve subsequent reviews.

Figure 3.5 Excerpt from a review letter.

Dear Reviewer:

The Editors have reached a decision regarding manuscript ID X entitled X which you recently reviewed for *Journal*. Below is a copy of the disposition letter sent to the author. Once again, we appreciate your valuable contributions to the peer review process.

Sincerely,
Editorial Office

Dear (Author),

Thank you for submitting your work to *Journal*. We would like to inform you that the review of your manuscript, X, entitled X, is now complete.

Please find included the reviews of your manuscript. After careful consideration of the reviewers' comments and a discussion of your manuscript in our editorial meeting, we regret to inform you that we have decided not to accept your manuscript for publication in *Journal*.

The reviewers noted that the topic of your manuscript was interesting. However, they also noted concerns with the tone of the manuscript, the lack of data to support your assertions, and the lack of context.

The reviewers have written very insightful and detailed comments. They are encouraging and provide many suggestions for possible directions for your work. We hope these reviews are helpful in the further development of your ideas.

Figure 3.5 (Continued)

Thank you for considering *Journal* as a possible outlet for your manuscript.

Sincerely,
Editors

Reviewers' Comments to Author:

Reviewer: 1

I quite enjoyed this ms and I believe that with revision, it should be published in *Journal*.

The scenario you provide makes your point about the potentiality of too much instruction killing the enjoyment of reading a text. But it is overstated and also somewhat misleading in that you are comparing one mode with another and one context with another. I cannot imagine a teacher in a "film" or video class not helping students develop meta-knowledge of the movie or video when necessary, just as a teacher in a literacy class would with texts. And I cannot imagine a librarian using these instructional strategies as children or adults sit in a library reading a book. So while I agree with your caution about overusing strategies, I believe you need to make the point in a more nuanced way.

On page 5, you say, "X...:" But you do not provide an example of a strategy that a teacher might use here.

On page 6 in critiquing teachers' use of X you suggest "Why not simply ask what we really want to know—What genre is the text?" Here again, you need to elaborate why a teacher would do this. What would students learn from the question and how will they benefit as readers?

As I read your ms, the question that keeps popping up for me is, "Why would teachers do what is being described here?" To me, that is a fundamental question that you as the

Figure 3.5 (Continued)

author need to address. Without that information, I interpret your text as teacher bashing and I am convinced that this is not an interpretation that you want readers to make. So some questions that arose for me:

- What is the larger socio-political culture in which these teachers are working?

- If factors and ideologies outside teachers' control largely dictate what they do, what advice would you have for them in terms of changing pedagogical practices, in an era of accountability, standardization and so forth?

- What is the influence of colleges and teacher education programs in universities on the pedagogical practices of their students/graduates? (I believe you indicate you supervise student teachers.)

- And what do teachers have to say about what they do?

To reiterate, you have identified an important issue, but I feel that you need to address it in a more contextualized manner.

Reviewer: 2

(There are no comments.)

Reviewer: 3

As this author suggests, teachers' implementation of good ideas often drifts from the research guidelines that support them. On other occasions, practices become popular without sufficient empirical warrant. These possibilities are important to note. This author ventures into that arena. The approach that she uses to address these ideas inserts several concerns about the appropriateness of this manuscript for *Journal*.

The author begins with a clever comparison between viewing a movie and the practices that some teachers use

Figure 3.5 (Continued)

to promote comprehension. This hypothetical scenario holds the potential to make poignant points. Instead, the author too quickly turns to a one-sided depiction of the unintended consequences that might emerge. And, any practice can be misused or overused. The author then singles out a few practices for further criticism as opposed to a more objective consideration of good things that can go awry. The objections to Question the Author is but one example of the author raising points without fully explaining the concern or selecting pieces to disdain and setting aside other pieces to value. Certainly, current scholarship brings the importance of agency and the importance of a reader to hold it. Attributes such as action, capability, choice and independence are valued. However, even this does not come without a second possibility: agency presupposes patiency, capability presupposes incapability, choice presupposes necessity and independence presupposes dependency.

Other parts of the manuscript come with questions. For example, what does "prevention rather than best practice" mean? How does "learning to read is to read literature" coincide with the necessity for students to read (and write) like historians, scientists, mathematicians, and literary theorists? Why does an expectation for a reader to take an efferent stance compete with an aesthetic one? Rosenblatt noted the appropriateness of both depending upon a reader's purpose.

Throughout this manuscript, the author often uses phrases such as "I have found" as warrant for her suggestions and stances. While personal experiences matter, they offer insufficient support for a proposal intended for a wider audience.

On a less important note, the author needs to carefully reread this manuscript for grammatical oversights. A full attention to APA format is also needed.

Overall, this is an important and timely topic.

Another way to keep learning is to review as many examples as possible to help develop useful phrases, lists of things to look for, and ways to gently note areas of both strength and weakness in a manuscript. As noted previously, useful review comments accomplish two purposes: (1) they help inform the editor's final decision on the manuscript's appropriateness for the journal, and (2) they offer insights for the author to understand the strengths and potential improvements for the manuscript. The sample reviews in this chapter's appendix offer initial guidance for ways to make points that do not sidestep making difficult points but also do not fall prey to sounding overly judgmental and harsh. The samples demonstrate the idea noted previously that reviews differ based on the expectations of the journal as well as the type of manuscript; they address a variety of outlets, formats, and audiences and include a research manuscript, a teaching recommendation, a full-length practical manuscript, and a theoretical piece. Reading this combination of examples and noting the types of reviews, the ideas that are presented, the delivery of them, and the final recommendation that each review supports can solidify an understanding of the content and wording of a review.

The Roles of Technology

Especially in the 21st century, technology plays a central role in reviewing manuscripts. An invitation to review typically comes by an e-mail in which editorial board members have a chance to accept or decline an invitation from the editor (see an example in Figure 3.6). If accepting, a follow-up e-mail will direct you to the journal's on-line site. With some exceptions, editorial boards use an on-line site where reviewers read and evaluate an assigned article. While some editorial boards meet at annual conventions to have a face-to-face exchange, offer suggestions for improving the system or the quality of the reviews, or simply thank people for their contributions, the ongoing work is done online.

Figure 3.6 Sample review invitation.

Dear Reviewer,

Manuscript IN 15-ES-161 titled "Reading Science for Meaning" has been submitted to this journal. I wonder if you might be available and willing to review this manuscript? The abstract appears at the end of this letter. I would need to receive your evaluation within 4 weeks. I would appreciate if you register your response to this invitation using one of the links below:

Agreed: https://urldefense.proofpoint.com/yes
Declined: https://urldefense.proofpoint.com/no

I realize that our expert reviewers greatly contribute to the high standards of the journal, and I thank you for considering this invitation.

Listing Reviewing on a CV or Résumé

As with all service contributions, you want to include editorial board memberships on your vita so you receive acknowledgement for them. No formal requirements exist for their format; however, a helpful entry will have a consistent organization that aligns with other sections of the vita and provides salient information. These three suggestions align with generally accepted formats:

- Use a caption such as "Related Professional Experience" and list "Editorial activities" as a subheading under it or use a caption such as "Professional Service" with "Service to the Discipline" as its subheading.
- Regardless of the headings, list all journal editorial positions, your role (e.g., editor, co-editor, editorial board member, reviewer), and your dates of involvement.
- Start the list with the most recent position if applicable.

Figure 3.7 Vita entries for reviewing.

Professional Activities

Journal Editorships

The Reading Journal, 2013–2015
Reading With Children, 2007–2010

Editorial Boards

Reading Teacher, 2010–present
Yearbook of the Association of Literacy Educators and Researchers, 2005–present
Journal of Literacy Research, 2013–present
Journal of Educational Research, 2005–present
Research in Middle Level Education Online, 2000–present
Middle Grades Research Journal, 2012–2015
Journal of Teacher Education, 2007–present
Childhood Education, 2000–2005

Figure 3.7 provides an example of how reviewing might be listed on a vita. From this combination of editorial board memberships, we learn about this person's combination of professional interests (literacy, research, middle grades, and teacher education) and the progression of various editorial opportunities (from a practitioner journal to research-oriented outlets). The continuity of contributions also becomes apparent, as indicated by the years of service. These attributes become important to evidence the coherence and continuity of a service role.

Conclusion

The benefits of serving as a reviewer are many. These include both professional and personal benefits (e.g., adding service to the profession, which in turn contributes to promotion and tenure accomplishments, enhancing an understanding of the attributes that make a manuscript ready for publication, and improving the quality of one's own writing). A reviewer also must be generous with his or her time and committed to meeting the demands expected of an editorial board member. If this interest remains, the following guidelines solidify the points made across this chapter for effective membership on an editorial board:

- Target a journal of interest.
- Obtain the information about this journal and carefully analyze your strengths and needs in light of this journal's orientation and expectation.
- Update your vita to present your related experiences in the most beneficial way.
- Submit your application as noted by the journal.
- If accepted, then pay careful attention to the due date for your review, and apply the suggestions from this chapter to write a review that helps the editor and the author (e.g., be straightforward, kind, and coherent).
- If denied, continue to strengthen the experiences that would better position a fit.

Recommended Resources

- American Psychological Association. *Guidelines for reviewing manuscripts for training and education in professional psychology.* Available from www.apa.org/pubs/journals/tep/reviewer-guidelines.aspx

This site divides its recommendations into five sections: confidential communication, conflict of interest, writing a review, publication recommendation, and narrative evaluation. Their brevity and specificity make them a helpful resource around these important aspects.

- Bakanic, V., McPhail, C., & Simon, R. J. (1987). The manuscript review and decision-making process. *American Sociological Review*, 631–642.

  This article empirically identifies the areas that influence an editor's decision for accepting a manuscript.

- Baruch, Y., Sullivan, S., & Schepmyer, H. (2006). *Winning reviews: A guide for evaluating scholarly writing*. London; Palgrave.

  Winning Reviews expands this chapter's content into a full-length book, with detailed tips and complete examples.

- Lovejoy, T. I., Revenson, T. A., & France, C. R. (2011). Reviewing manuscripts for peer-review journals: A primer for novice and seasoned reviewers. *Annals of Behavioral Medicine*, *42*(1), 1–13.

  This article from the field of medicine provides suggestions especially appropriate for novice reviewers to build their understanding of the review process and the attributes of a quality review.

Guided Practice

1. Read the excerpts in Figure 3.5. Determine where the reviewers agree and disagree. Why might this be? Also, consider what comments from Reviewer 2 might have added to the review process. Why is it important for all reviewers to complete their tasks?

2. If the journal allows, find a colleague who currently reviews for a journal of interest to you. Share with this colleague your aspirations to also review for this journal and ask if you could do a "shadow" review of a manuscript with him or her. This process would entail receiving a copy of the

manuscript, drafting a review, and then comparing it with the one your colleague writes. The final step would be to arrange a conversation to compare your reviews.

3. Collect a list of guidelines for editorial review board membership, examine the fit between them and your background, and submit applications to those most suited for your interests and current experiences.

4. Consult your promotion and tenure guidelines (or those for a university where you would like to work) to understand the role of review board membership for promotion and tenure.

References

Lee, A. S. (1995). Guidelines for reviewing manuscripts for training and education in professional psychology. *Journal of Operations Management, 13,* 87–92.

Provenzale, J. M., & Stanley, P. J. (2006). A systematic guide to reviewing a manuscript. *American Journal of Roentgeneology, 34*(2), 848–854.

Shulman, L. S. (1997). Disciplines of inquiry in education: A new overview. In R. M. Jaeger (Ed.), *Complementary methods for research in education* (2nd ed., pp. 3–29). Washington, DC: American Educational Research Association.

Sample 1

These authors' manuscript crisscrosses an array of timely and important topics. They coalesce around an overall intention to address the plight of culturally and linguistically diverse students. However, within that overall intention, their purpose becomes less clear. This inability to build a central and focused argument lessens an enthusiasm for the publication of this work at this time.

The abstract hints at a less-than-clear focus. This begins with the audience and concept of importance. The authors move from the dispositions of pre-service teachers to the composition of the teaching population to the inadequacy of teacher educators. Each of these groups and points matter. However, if the authors intend a simultaneous attention to them, then they must meet this ambitious goal. Instead, the content comments on the edges of them while giving primary attention to their teaching circumstances.

Then, the authors describe their theoretical framework in terms of critical race theory. This choice makes sense for the topics that they address—individually and collectively. However, this commitment implies that it will permeate future comments and outlooks. In subsequent sections, the authors make important links to existing scholarship. However, at best, the authors tap into a critical race theory framework indirectly rather than directly.

In putting forward their ideas, the authors make many assertions. Too often, and as they acknowledge, they remain speculative. Resorting to "possible explanations" instead of empirical verification lessens the warrant for their claims.

Other pieces combine to insert additional reservations. For example, the authors reference a teacher educator's journal without explaining the nature or purpose of its compilation. Its use in this instance raises concerns. How can it include exact quotes from teachers? How does the use of excerpts address the possibility for selectivity that proves a point without capturing the overall essence of the ideas captured across time? How do the authors address an ongoing expectation to address subjectivity in scholarly work?

Finally, the authors need to clearly establish the final point that they want their readers to hold. Is it the need of teacher educators to do more to address diversity? Is it a call for pre- and in-service teachers to do more to address diversity? Is it actually the delicate balances and interactions that occur within and across these groups? Or, and more in keeping with their final quote, is it a call to diversify the composition of teachers and teacher educators? Connective tissue exists between these various areas. The authors need to do more to provide it. Simply stated, the authors' ideas deserve a powerful presentation and a memorable ending note. In its present form, it falls short of these hopes and possibilities.

Sample 2

I found this manuscript very difficult to read and comprehend. This was in part because of word choices and organization but also due to lack of information, overgeneralizations, and some missing sections that I expected to see. Some of these issues are exemplified below:

- The abstract notes that the study is of the effects (implying experiment) of X technologies (all of them?) on Y. It's not.
- Many focal terms are not described well or even at all. These include "informal" (in one place it states that classrooms are informal, which contradicts the rest of the literature), "affordance" (many different definitions are given, some that contradict or are unrelated), "Web 2.0," "situated learning," "up-to-date personal experiences," "media technologies," and others. In addition, the author uses a definition of "affordance" from another field—a definition from a more closely related field is needed. In line 55 the author seems to indicate that technology that documents is Web 2.0, but that's Web 1.0. On page 6, web-based learning is equated (I think) with Web 2.0, but not all Web is Web 2.0, certainly.
- That learners found Web 2.0 motivating is not new, nor is research based on survey/perceptions. If the author can explain why the situation already explored in the literature might be different in [their country], that could fill a gap, but no reason is given.
- The author treats "Web 2.0" as a single entity throughout the manuscript, but it certainly isn't. I imagine that the students only use a small subset of Web 2.0 tools, and these need to be explicated for the study to have meaning.
- The author states that affordances make technologies easy to learn. Not necessarily so.

- Misstatements/overgeneralizations include:
  - o "technologies … afford learning motivation" (inaccurate use of "afford," lines 31–35)
  - o Due to interaction, students "become active, self-motivated" (they MAY, but they don't always. lines 44–46)
  - o "Through life-long experience with technology, young students are confident" (Not ALL of them have or are. These kinds of statements, which occur regularly throughout the paper, need to be qualified). Here are a couple more—"Web 2.0 activities support learning" (well they *might/can*), "Web 2.0 technologies offer a stimulating" (*sometimes* they do), "Web 2.0 tools link minds … leading to joint knowledge creation" (That's the intent, but do they ALL?).
  - o "vital for educators to find out how and why youngsters learn" (First, this presupposes that they do, without evidence, and second, it suggests that this manuscript will explore this, but it doesn't).
  - o "their daily learning culture as developed by Web 2.0 media" (What does this mean? In several other cases Web 2.0 is anthropomorphized and given the power to act that it doesn't have.)
  - o "Twitter can transform social networking into educational networking (meaning?) because of three features." Just because Twitter has these affordances doesn't mean that it can be educational without someone guiding learners to complete "educational" tasks! The role of some kind of guidance is really overlooked in this paper—perhaps a better description of informal learning environments would help here, too.
  - o In lines 4–6 on p. 5, the author implies (I think) that the teacher replying to tweets is "informal learning." How?

- Page 6 seems to indicate that technology use is the same as affordance, which of course it's not. I'm not sure how these two ideas relate. On the same page, the author claims that "web-based learning is mostly social and peer based." Not true most places in the world, where Web 1.0 generally predominates.

- I got lost in the part about limitations and challenges—access and funding aren't affordances of a technology, so it's hard to say what the point of this part is. In this same section, the author talks about assigning an "online compulsory assignment," but I'm not sure how that would be informal learning.

- The theoretical framework section is too complex. First, there are no cites for the initial mentions of situated learning or affordance theory and no explanations of these theories, including components included in the framework. It says that "artifacts are mediated" but arrows in the model show relationship, not mediation. It also talks about collective motives and intentions in the text, but I'm not sure where these are in the model. It's just not clear, particularly the summary on p. 9 that doesn't really seem to relate to the theories or model at all. It could just be semantics—cleaning up the language use could make the difference.

- Methodology is missing sections. Where is the context, details about the participants, research questions, survey questions, data sources, etc.?

- Most grievously, the author contends that the study is mixed methods. It is not. Collecting numeric data via survey doesn't make a study quantitative. Under a quantitative paradigm, experimental or quasi-experimental research is carried out. The current study is qualitative, supported by numeric data. A manuscript with this huge error cannot be published in a major journal.

- There are many problems in the discussion section, from making assertions without data to making assertions that don't seem to match the data. These are too numerous to write here.
- Overall, there are no real findings as they are stated currently. Page 14 implies correlation where none was conducted, and no examples are given to show the data. A learning measure is also implied on p. 14, but none was given.
- There is no explanation of how often participants used Web 2.0, which tools, and why. This information would help explain and give context to the otherwise overgeneralized results.
- Finally, there is no limitations section, and studies based on self-report have many limitations.

Overall, I think that a lot of rewording might make this paper less opaque. Simple is good!

Sample 3

As the author states, many older readers have difficulty with the longer words that often appear in their assigned and self-selected texts. The author proposes a strategy for addressing this challenge. However, several concerns prevent a recommendation for its wider dissemination.

First, the author does not place his or her suggestions within a theoretical framework. Without stating this, the focus on accurately saying words appears to suggest an emphasis at the word level. If correct pronunciation captures this authors' view of reading, then the author needs to position that claim within a well-articulated point of reference. If the ultimate goal is comprehension, then the author needs to position the accurate pronunciation of words within this goal. Regardless, a theoretical framework would allow a reader insight into this author's orientation toward reading and reading well.

Second, the author provides information about doing the proposed strategy but fails to identify any scholarship that directly supports its use. Especially in today's climate, teachers crave ideas that are practical and important for their students and also hold warrant.

In addition, the author underestimates the potential to address the concern of those long words by using syllabication and phonics. Several misconceptions get in the way. For example, syllabication applies to root words—not words with affixes attached. Then, phonics applies to syllables—not whole words. Students who understand those pieces can more ably capitalize on the generalizations about syllabications and phonics. Relatively simple understandings such as these apply: any vowel can represent a schwa sound, and vowels usually represent a schwa in an unaccented syllable. The key point with any of this is a teacher's ability to fully explain the possibilities and limitations of a word's examination to infer its pronunciation and a reader's ability to use approximations to obtain accuracy.

Finally, the author makes no mention of the role of oral language in settling on correct pronunciation. In many instances, a reader who incorrectly pronounces a word encountered while reading can combine the context with his or her oral language to correctly say an unknown word.

Overall, the complexity of this author's suggestions, the absence of direct support for their effectiveness, and the availability of better-known and documented options reduce the need for offering this as a Teaching Tip.

Sample 4

Responding appropriately to students as they read aloud remains important and timely. As this author notes, too often the student hears an encouragement to "sound it out." The author offers suggestions for moving beyond what the author considers an overused and often less-than-helpful exhortation. However, several reservations prevent a nod for its publication in *XXX*.

Of most importance, the author falls short of introducing a fresh perspective to these recommendations. In general, the *XXX* audience brings a level of sophistication that these recommendations underrate. The author's compilation of references further underscores the length of time that these ideas have been known. Specifically, only two references have a publication date beyond 1999, while four citations appear before 1970. Certainly, historical pieces and seminal research matter. However, new work demands new news.

Then, part of crafting a manuscript includes identifying an audience. Here, the author seems conflicted. Initially, the author addressed parents, moves to teachers, references clinicians, and then addresses literacy coaches. While the suggestions might address these various roles, the unique variations they introduce warrant attention.

In addition, the author needs to do more to substantiate his or her claims. Too often the author simply states, "research suggests." At other times, ideas and suggestions seem to stem from personal ideas and beliefs rather than having a foothold in existing scholarship.

Finally, the author might consider strengthening the conclusion. If rereading is the big idea for this work, then the author needs to do more to have it take center stage. If not, then placing it as the final word seems to set aside the other ideas presented in this manuscript.

In the end, and as initially stated, this paper does not seem to fit the expectations as a manuscript for *XXX*. Revisiting and revising it might lead to a piece appropriate for *XXX*.

Sample 5

Comments

With the international attention that so many areas receive, the title is misleading. Specifically mentioning the theory (and not its acronym) would prevent someone from thinking that this was about the region of X. The author cites a number of factors that contribute to participation in extracurricular activities and then settles on one theorist, X. More needs to be done to establish the reasoning behind the selection of X's theory, one that is 30 years old. This explanation should directly address the theory's relevance for this investigation in light of existing scholarship and its placement as an exclusive focus of this work. Then, specificity across the paper would add clarity (e.g., "one of X's primary personality types" instead of stating it, "on the basis of X's assumption"—What is it?). While the author previously mentions this information, its placement in the manuscript does not reduce ambiguity when referenced at later points.

When turning to the particulars of this study, oversights exist, questions arise, and concerns remain. First, the purpose of this investigation drifts. Its initial purpose suggests "using" Holland's theory, but it seems to be more about testing the theory rather than using it. A thin line might exist between these two purposes, but the author needs to clearly address it. In addition, the author needs to serve two goals in the sections leading up to the explanation of methods: a traditional literature review and a thorough explanation of Holland's theory. These areas relate, and making those connections matters, but each must receive thorough attention. As presented, the author moves quickly from one thing to another, which contributes to a thin account of what is known, a superficial account of Holland's theory, and a lack of clarity about the relationships across these two pieces of information.

Often, empirical work becomes necessary to substantiate ideas that appear logical but might or might not have evidence to verify it. This work falls into that category with one notable exception: X's work is used to verify X's work. This seems to limit the appearance of an objective investigation. The findings result in a rather basic and uninspired claim: Students' interests align with their preferences for after-school activities. The author needs to do more to position this basic claim as providing a major contribution to existing scholarship. The creation and use of X also lacks depth. If X created it, then his tool is being used to verify his tool. Certainly, he would have considered congruence between the two tools, thus lessening an independent look at either X or X. They come together. The use of a "X code expert" further taints the findings. A person often finds what they look to find, and someone linked to Holland's theory might be prone to stretch a look at the data to find the hoped-for fit. These decisions inform the statistical findings and come with suspicion.

In the end, the author lays claim to a rather mundane finding that does little to move the field forward. Students will do what students want to do. Ask them. Provide their responses. Then, investigate whether that responsiveness results in higher attendance or achievement. That finding would inform the field around the question that holds center stage: student achievement.

4

WRITING REVIEWS OF PUBLISHED ACADEMIC BOOKS, TRADE BOOKS, AND MEDIA

From an academic book review:

> Evans's introduction and Chapter 1 provide an excellent rationale for looking at teacher research in a variety of contexts. He efficiently uses the existing research to support and explain the pedagogical assumptions underlying the authors' work in the book and provides background on their teaching settings. While doing so, he points out fallacies under which the CALL and technology education communities have been working and conducting research. He concludes that the teaching methodology, rather than the medium alone, is the crucial factor in learning.
>
> (Egbert, 2010, p. 223)

Overview

In Chapter 3, we discussed reviewing journal articles and other academic manuscripts prior to publication. Early-career faculty might find it too difficult or time consuming to perform effective journal manuscript reviews until they obtain more experience with research, and journals often wait until a scholar publishes in them to ask that scholar to serve on the editorial board. In the meantime, however, those who want to can practice reviewing skills and publish by performing other kinds of reviews of resources such as newly published professional books, trade books that might be used in education (meaning books that are published by a popular press, not textbooks), and software, videos, and other types of education media. There are many great opportunities for graduate and other students of education to review these types of media, too. Unlike manuscript reviews, these reviews are written for a broad audience, published in a journal, and carry the author's name.

The excerpt from Egbert's review of a published text shows how part of the text review is often a summary of the main ideas in the book's chapters. This is different, and perhaps easier, than writing a review of a research paper that requires analysis of its arguments and methods. Belcher (n.d.) adds that book (and media) reviews are "the easiest and quickest route to publication" (p. 1), but, as we note in what follows, not all reviews carry the same weight for tenure and other personal and institutional purposes.

This chapter addresses:

- Choosing a resource to review
- Understanding review guidelines
- Guidelines for writing a review
- Listing published reviews on a CV or résumé
- The role of technology in reviewing

Choosing a Resource to Review

The first step to conducting a review is choosing what to review. The choice should depend on (1) what is valued by the reviewer's institution; (2) what interests and knowledge the reviewer has; (3) how much time can be allotted to the task, and (4) the reviewer's ability to meet the journal's review guidelines. These guidelines are discussed in what follows.

Review Value

First, potential reviewers should consider that some universities will "count" refereed reviews of professional books in a tenure packet, while others will not count any kind of review. Credit for trade book reviews might be more likely to be granted to faculty at institutions focused on teaching and those whose job encourages them to contribute to the scholarship of pedagogy. A media review can span both contexts (professional and trade), depending on the forum in which it is published and how it is reviewed. Reviewers should explore what kinds of credit their institution might give them for a review and whether the time spent on the review is worth whatever the work and personal benefits might be.

Reviewer Expertise

Second, unlike journal manuscript reviews, which are usually requested by an editor based on expertise and experience, books and media to review can often be chosen by the reviewer. For example, the *Review of Higher Education* guidelines note:

> In order to have your review considered, first contact the editor via email to ensure that the [material] has not been reviewed or that it is not currently under review. In addition, the editor maintains a small library of books not yet reviewed that may be of interest to potential reviewers.
> (www.press.jhu.edu/journals/review_of_
> higher_education/guidelines.html)

However, expertise and experience still play a role. For example, scholars at a research-focused university might look for academic books around ideas in their area of expertise to review; this allows them to read up on the newest published ideas in the field while also gaining a publication. Educators can also review in order to gain new knowledge, but some journals will require a statement of expertise ahead of time, such as the journal *Education Review*, which notes in its journal guidelines: "Please know that we are selective with regard to both the qualifications of reviewers and the quality of their reviews ... Part of the form, common to review requests, is for the reviewer to *describe your interest in this book and qualifications for reviewing it*" (http://edrev.asu.edu/index.php/ER/about/submissions).

Aside from professional books, educators who use (or want to use) trade books in their classrooms might want to add a review to one of the trade book review sites or a more practice-based journal. Reviews can range from full-length trade books such as *The Physics of Star Trek* (Krauss, 2007) to children's books such as *Yo! Yes?* (Raschka, 2007) used in discipline-area and teacher education classes. In addition, educators who have access to and use technology can consider contributing their expertise to the review of new technologies. Although it is certainly possible to review outside one's experience and expertise, it might not allow for the review to be compared to other similar resources or to have the benefit of background knowledge an effective review relies on.

Allotting Time

Third, academic book reviews will often take longer to conduct than reviews of other types of media, given the intensity and the length of the resource. Children's trade books might be reviewed in a short amount of time, while young adult and adult literature might take longer. The time to complete a media review will vary by the content, length, and type of media. The reviewer must consider the balance between time spent and benefits of reviewing.

Understanding Review Guidelines

Many academic journals do not have a review section, and some do not accept unsolicited reviews even if they do. However, it is sometimes possible to ask to complete a review. For example, the journal *Education Review* provides these instructions:

> Take the following link where you can fill out a Request to Review after scanning the books currently available for review: **Request to Review...** **Choose the book you wish to review** in which appears the author and title of a single book and a list of all the books available for review will appear.
>
> (www.edrev.info/contribute.html)

In all cases, a completed review does not imply that the review will be published by the journal; the review editor typically reserves the right to ask for edits or to reject the review outright. The *Journal of Educational Foundations* states, "Our policy is to assign books to specific reviewers. Please note that assignments do not guarantee publication."

In order to make sure the work that goes into the review is rewarded by publication, it is essential for potential reviewers of any type of published media to clearly understand the guidelines for the selected publication forum. These can vary quite widely from publication to publication as to review length and contents, but information can usually be found in the "Information for Authors" or "Submission Guidelines" of the journal or its website. Figures 4.1 and 4.2 provide a list of sample journals and other forums that accept reviews and some of the review guidelines.

Overall, then, the idea is to first determine whether a review is something worth doing, whether for personal or professional gain. Then make sure the book or media meets your interest and expertise level and that you have time to do it. Finally,

Figure 4.1 Sample of forums for professional book and media reviews.

Forum	Accepts	Length	Guidelines URL
Issues in Teacher Education	Book and media reviews	700–1,500 words	www1.chapman.edu/ ITE/public_html/Docs/ BMRGAug.pdf
TESL-EJ	Books	1,500–2,000 words	www.tesl-ej.org/ wordpress/ submission-information/ review-policy/
Journal of Sustainability Education	Book and media	500–3,000	www.jsedimensions. org/wordpress/aboutus/ submission-guidelines/
Hispania	Books and media	500–1,000	www.aatsp. org/?page=hispania
Journal of Student Affairs Research and Practice	Books and media	Up to 1,200 words	www.naspa.org/ publications/journals/ journal-of-student-affairs-research-and-practice/guidelines
Mid-Western Educational Researcher	Books and media	5–10 pages	www.mwera.org/MWER/ info-for-authors.html
Journal of Chemical Education	Books and media	800 words	http://pubs.acs.org/ paragonplus/submission/ jceda8/jceda8_authguide. pdf

in choosing what to review and for which education forum, be aware of the journal's or other forum's policy on reviews, including who might perform them and how to get permission to do one. The subsequent step is to understand what should comprise the contents of the review, discussed next.

Figure 4.2 Sample of forums for trade book and other types of media reviews.

Forum	Accepts	Process	Guidelines URL
TESOL Journal	Reviews of teaching materials, teacher resources, technology resources, and creative works	Secure permission from resource publisher first	http://onlinelibrary.wiley.com/jour nal/10.1002/(IS SN)1949–3533/ homepage/ ForAuthors.html
Journal of Technology and Teacher Education	Courseware evaluations	None specified	www.aace.org/ publish/begin/
Journal of Media Literacy Education	Books, curriculum materials, multimedia, online resources	Contact professional resources editor	http:// digitalcommons.uri. edu/jmle/policies. html
Journal of Student Affairs Research and Practice	Media features and reviews; Internet resources, blogs, newsletters, film/ video, presentation materials	Invited by associate editor	www.naspa.org/ publications/ journals/journal- of-student-affairs- research-and- practice/guidelines
The Rocky Mountain Review	Trade books, resource books	Check the list at http://rmmla. innoved.org/ ereview/queue. asp	http://rmmla. innoved.org/ereview/ reviews.asp

Guidelines for Reviews

It should be taken for granted that reviews should be free of surface errors, be formatted to the requirements of the journal or other publishing outlet, and contain the expected content.

However, the content of reviews of different kinds of materials for different publication outlets might vary widely. This difference is best seen by comparing requirements among representative journals for each of the three types of review materials (professional books, trade books, and media) as presented in what follows.

Professional Books

Most reviews start with details of the resource being reviewed. For example, common to many book reviews, *Education Review* expects that "Every review should begin by citing the book or books to be reviewed, with full bibliographic information including authors (please include first names), copyright date, full title including any subtitle, place of publication, publisher, number of pages, ISBN Number. Pricing information is not needed" (www.edrev.info/contribute.html). On the other hand, *Review of Higher Education* does expect the price to be included, and both journals ask reviewers to use APA format in their reviews.

After the details, the required review content typically includes some kind of overview of the text and a critical evaluation. For example, additional information provided for reviewers who want to review for the *Journal of Educational Foundations* notes that reviews "are intended to be as engaging, insightful, and well-written as those articles that emerge from the referee process. Book reviews are also designed to provide readers with both accurate descriptions of the books being reviewed and thoughtful evaluations of their meaning, utility, and relevance ... as well as discuss the book's likely contribution and value to academics and policymakers" ((http://intraweb.stockton.edu/eyos/page.cfm?siteID=144& pageID=9).

Where not explicitly stated in the review guidelines, a book review can follow the useful content outline from the Massey University Online Writing and Learning Link (OWLL) at http://owll.massey.ac.nz/assignment-types/book-review.php. Among its clear description of the review process, it explains that:

> A book review is a critical assessment of a book. It describes and evaluates the quality and significance of a book and does not merely summarize the content.
>
> Identify:
>
> - Author's content and purpose
> - Structure
> - Audience
>
> Evaluate:
>
> - Accuracy
> - Up-to-datedness of the information
> - The sources used to justify the author's stance
>
> Respond:
>
> - What issues does it raise?
> - What issues are omitted?
> - The effect of the book
> - Your recommendation

Because guidelines might be specific to the publishing outlet, reviewers must read carefully not only the submission guidelines that describe who might write a review and how to get permission but also those that describe what the editor or referees are looking for in a review. If these are not included in the submission guidelines, a suggestion to contact the review editor by e-mail or other means often is, and we recommend that reviewers take advantage of any information the review editor can offer.

Trade Book Reviews

Like reviews of professional books, trade book reviews typically start with details about the book itself, and, also like professional book reviews, they can be different lengths and have different content depending on the publishing forum. For example, *TESOL Journal* requires a "description of how they have been successfully used in the classroom," while a journal in the same field, *TESL-EJ*, asks reviewers to "give an overview of the book, its purpose, and audience. Then incorporate summaries and/or details of specific sections as part of your assessment" (www. tesl-ej.org/wordpress/submission-information/review-policy/). Classroom use might be included but is not required. On the other hand, while *The Rocky Mountain Review* does not provide detailed guidelines for review content, reading several of the published reviews, such as the one in Figure 4.3, can provide the reviewer with information on expectations.

Figure 4.3 Sample trade book review by L. Pritchett (2013). *Rocky Mountain e-Review.*

Barbara Richardson. *Tributary, A novel.* Torrey, Utah: Torrey House Press, 2012. 352 p.

Laura Pritchett
University of Northern Colorado

Mormonism is hot these days: everything from Mitt Romney's faith careening into national politics to the Broadway hit *Book of Mormon.* Add to that mix a new historical novel by Colorado author Barbara Richardson, whose book *Tributary* takes on the incomplete history of the Mormon religion. Set in a Utah Territory in the mid-1800s, the novel follows Clair Martin, a misfit in a Mormon frontier town, and shows what polygamy feels like from inside the fold. Her life becomes a

Figure 4.3 (Continued)

quiet revolution as she untangles herself from a religion and culture she finds wanting. While the writing is superb, it's the plot that offers the greatest strength of this book. Simply put: the novel does what art should do, which is to show us our lives with renewed clarity and better insight. *Tributary* takes the incomplete history and mythos of the West to task, and instead shows us some of the far more interesting and unexplored stories of American West—Mormonism, racism, women who don't need marriage or men. Beautifully written and engaging, this is a story of one woman and her refusal to cave into societal norms in order to seek her own difficult and inspired path.

The greatest problem with literature set in the Western US, of course, is the lure of falling into the Western myth. In most of our past literary history, the West has been portrayed one way: Men were the focus; they were quiet and stoic, they had a bunch of broken dreams, and they sure as hell couldn't be scared of camping alone at night. There was an absence of minorities or women, except to use them as characters who reflected something about the man.

Big changes have occurred, of course. We evolved. We quit talking about gunplay and instead started talking about other compelling stories. We quit being so romantic and nostalgic. New voices became part of our literary dialogue: voices by minorities and women, for instance, who had characters way more complicated and interesting than the single silent unafraid cowboy.

This book is a prime example of breaking the pattern of romanticizing the West. In that regard, Richardson, whose Mormon ancestors settled the northern Salt Lake Valley, is as brave as her protagonist—both are trying to capture a truer and richer version of what life was like for those outside the center of power—Native Americans, blacks, women—and to thus offer a more complete portrait of life in the American West.

Clearly, the expectation of this journal is a short summary of the text, followed by a lengthier examination of how it fits into the canon and what its strengths and weaknesses might be. To determine what to include and in what manner to do so, the reviewer should read not only the submission guidelines but also previously published reviews in the chosen forum.

Media Reviews

Depending on the journal or other publishing outlet, media can refer to a wide variety of resources including films, Ted Talks, software, websites, blogs, and social media or other applications. As noted, it is important for reviewers to know about exactly which media their target outlet publishes reviews. Media reviews often require the same publishing details as other types of reviews, while also possibly including a version number (software), original publication date and latest update (website), and the name of the author, the site, and the platform (blogs and other media).

While some media reviews might only ask for reviewers to relate their experience with the media, refereed media and book reviews might also require a theoretical or literature-based framework in which to ground the evaluation. For example, *Language Learning and Technology* requests that:

> Reviews should provide a constructive critique of the book/software and include references to theory and research...They should also include specific ideas for classroom implementation and suggestions for additional research...
>
> (http://llt.msu.edu/contrib.html#articles)

In meeting these requirements, Egbert (2004) reviewed a software package intended to help second-language learners improve their pronunciation in English. She based her review on criteria culled from pronunciation research. Figure 4.4 shows how she constructed her review based on this literature; italics have been added to highlight the theoretical framework she used. The rest of this review can be found in the examples at the end of this chapter.

Figure 4.4 Excerpt from Egbert (2004).

To be able to speak and listen in a second language, it is clear that language learners need something other than just phonemic correctness. As or more important seems to be the ability to comprehend and produce in a near-native-like fashion aspects of pronunciation such as stress, intonation, rhythm, and pacing, and to use gestures and body language appropriately; in other words, to have both linguistic and sociolinguistic competence (Celce-Murcia, Brinton, & Goodwin, 1996; Florez, 1999). In many cases, however, pronunciation teaching still focuses on discrete phonemic awareness and production. For many reasons, this approach has been relatively ineffective to date (Boku, 1998; Donahue, 1999). Fraser (1999) notes that most language learners feel that pronunciation is a crucial part of language learning. Students believe the best way to improve their pronunciation is to practice, and many pronunciation experts agree that pronunciation teaching and learning must be situated in communicative contexts (Fraser, 1999; Levis, 1999; Otlowski, 1998; Wennerstrom, 1999) and help students to use metacognitive strategies in broader communication (Vitanova & Miller, 2002). Otlowski and Fraser (1999) concur with much of the current research that the goals of pronunciation teaching should be "developing functional intelligibility, communicability, increased self-confidence, the development of speech monitoring abilities and speech modification strategies for use beyond the classroom" (p. 3). In order to reach these goals, Morley (1991) and Fraser (1999) call for more emphasis on

Figure 4.4 (Continued)

individual learners' needs, supporting a learner-centered approach that involves authentic tasks and the use of peers and groups for interaction and feedback to help learners be critical listeners and develop the ability to notice and repair their own and others' errors. In this model, the role of the teacher is facilitator rather than error corrector or ultimate speech model. In the facilitator role, the teacher can offer various models, provide opportunities for practice, suggest specific techniques, and give encouragement and advice to learners as they work toward intelligibility. Morley (1991) calls this role the "speech coach." Fraser (2000) calls for "high quality, effective materials, especially computer-based materials with audio demonstrations, for learners of ESL pronunciation" (p. 2). Such materials, according to Chun (1998), would have to "present authentic speech samples within their cultural contexts and call learners' attention" (p. 73) to specific features. She also suggests that the software must support pair interaction and emphasize natural discourse.

In order to evaluate pronunciation software, we need to assess how well it teaches, or helps us to teach, in ways that will help students improve their pronunciation. This review is based on seven criteria taken from the literature described above. This list is not all-inclusive, nor does its use imply that the software must meet all of these conditions. These focused criteria, however, can serve as a basis for a discussion of the effectiveness of a software package for pronunciation teaching and learning (italics added).

Overall, the contents of media reviews probably vary most widely, but it is still important for reviewers of professional and trade books to make sure that they know what content is required.

Review-Writing Guidelines

Once the potential reviewer understands the content requirements of the journal for which the review is being prepared,
the focus should be on writing in the constructive, engaging,
and thoughtful manner requested by the publishing outlet.
Many of the guidelines are the same as those for journal manuscript reviewing, but others are not. To write an effective review,
reviewers should consider whichever of the following guidelines fit the publication outlet's requirements:

1. Read the book or use the media completely (not just a
   demo version). Try to become familiar with the purpose
   and content of the product and note any major issues, both
   positive and negative. Because the book or media product
   has already been published, it is not as important to report
   on surface errors in grammar and punctuation as it would
   be for a journal manuscript, but all the "big ideas" should
   be noted. (As needed, read other reviews to determine what
   the publisher understands these "big ideas" to consist of.)
2. If possible, use the product with the intended audience and
   take notes of their reactions, how they use the product, and
   what they think about it as they use it. This data can be used
   not only to report on classroom use but also to uncover
   strengths and weaknesses.
3. If needed (or furnished by the publication outlet), create
   or use a relevant theoretical framework, as Egbert does in
   the media review in the appendix to this chapter. (For more
   on creating theoretical frameworks, see Egbert & Sanden,
   2014 and 2015). Listing several principles against which
   to compare the product helps readers understand specifically why and how the product is being evaluated and to
   judge whether this evaluation is valid. For example, an
   educational software package might be evaluated according to the engagement principles of interest, application,

challenge/interest balance, authenticity, and social interaction, as noted in the literature.

4. Read or use the product a second time and create the foundation for a summary of each major section of the text or media that can then be synthesized. For both book and media reviews, an overall summary of the product typically comprises a full paragraph. From this paragraph, readers should be able to obtain a clear understanding of the purpose and content of the product.

5. For the second reading or use, note areas of interest, possible quotes, issues, and other items to comment on according to the chosen theoretical framework. Provide a short (a sentence or two) explanation of each of the evaluation principles and note, with details and locations, how the product addresses each principle. For example, if using the engagement principles to evaluate software, you might comment on whether the software includes opportunities for students to interact socially and, if so, what these opportunities are.

6. Conclude the review with a general statement of the product based on how it met the elements of the theoretical framework. This statement might read something like, "This media provides opportunities for social interaction and application, but it would most likely not interest the intended audience, and it does not provide a variety of levels of challenge." Then include an evaluation statement; "This book/media might best be used with (specific learners) who (specific abilities or interests). This product would not be appropriate for (some classroom practice)." Alternatively, the conclusion could restate the overall benefits and disadvantages of the product and provide ways to use it that could enhance student achievement. In other words, the conclusion should provide readers with a final statement that sums up the reviewer's understandings of the product.

The language of the review should be simple and jargon free enough for the reader to follow easily. Screen shots or quotes, if allowed, can also greatly facilitate readers' understandings of both the review and the product under review.

The Roles of Technology in Reviewing

As with the review of academic manuscripts, discussed in Chapter 3, most reviews of published works are submitted online, making Internet access a requirement for this type of service. In addition, reviews must be word processed, and, if screen shots or other visuals are used, software that can be used to capture and manipulate these graphics might be necessary. As technology use becomes more ubiquitous, even some of the books and media to be reviewed are digital, making Web access and perhaps a digital book reader imperative.

Listing Published Reviews on a CV or Résumé

Once the review has been published, there is one more important aspect of the review to consider, and that is how to cite it. The website for the *Publication Manual of the American Psychological Association, Sixth Edition* (2010; also known as the *APA Manual*) suggests the following format to cite a review:

> Schatz, B. R. (2000, November 17). Learning by text or context? [Review of the book *The social life of information*, by J. S. Brown & P. Duguid]. *Science, 290*, 1304. doi:10.1126/science.290.5495.1304

The APA website (www.apastyle.org/learn/faqs/reference-book-review.aspx) adds that:

- If the review is untitled, use the material in brackets as the title; retain the brackets to indicate that the material is a description of form and content, not a title.

- Identify the type of medium being reviewed in brackets (book, motion picture, television program, etc.).
- If the reviewed item is a book, include the author names after the title of the book, separated by a comma.
- If the reviewed item is a film, DVD, or other media, include the year of release after the title of the work, separated by a comma.

(APA, 2010)

MLA (Modern Language Association) style citations are double-spaced and indented after the first line, and the review citation includes different organization than APA. The Purdue OWL explains:

> To cite a review, include the title of the review (if available), then the abbreviation "Rev. of" for Review of and provide the title of the work (in italics for books, plays, and films; in quotation marks for articles, poems, and short stories). Finally, provide performance and/or publication information.
>
> (https://owl.english.purdue.edu/owl/resource/747/07/)

In other words, the style is:

> Review Author. "Title of Review (if there is one)." Rev. of Performance Title, by Author/Director/Artist. *Title of Periodical* day month year: page. Medium of publication.

Figure 4.5 shows how the citation from the previous paragraph would look in MLA format.

Figure 4.5 MLA citation format for book review.

Schatz, Brian. "Learning by text or context?" Rev. of *The social life of information*, by J. S. Brown & P. Duguid. *Science* 290 (2000): 1304. Print.

Information about other styles or adaptations of these styles can be found in style guides across the World Wide Web and in their print versions.

Conclusion

There are many reasons to review professional books, trade books, and/or media; these can include completing requirements for tenure, obtaining free materials, fulfilling a desire to support the field, and/or personal knowledge. Regardless of the reason for reviewing, following the guidelines in this chapter can lead to successful publication of a review. Guidelines are:

1. Choose carefully: The choice should depend on what is valued by the institution, what interests and expertise the reviewer has, and how much time can be allotted to the task. Weigh the benefits against time and rewards.
2. Check the journal you are targeting for whether it accepts reviews and to get an overview of format and length expectations for the review.
3. Understand content requirements for the review: Examine previously published reviews, read the review guidelines closely, and contact the review editor if necessary.
4. Tap other resources, like those in the Recommended Resources section, for additional information and support in writing the review.

Recommended Resources

- *Book Reviews*—The Writing Center. UNC College of Arts and Sciences. Available: http://writingcenter.unc.edu/handouts/book-reviews/.

This handout provides step-by-step instructions for writing the review from a critical perspective.

- *Writing Book Reviews.* Writing Tutorial Services, Indiana University, 2014. Available: www.indiana.edu/~wts/pamphlets/book_reviews.shtml.

  A short and sweet overview of how to write a review.

- *Writing a Book Review.* The Purdue Online Writing Lab (OWL), 2015. Available: https://owl.english.purdue.edu/owl/resource/704/01/

  This resource includes sections called "Before You Read," "As You Read," "When You Are Ready to Write," and "Revising."

Guided Practice

1. Look at the similarities and differences among the example reviews below. What can you discern about the requirements for these reviews? Find the publications online and check the submission guidelines. What did you learn from this task?
2. Practice writing citations for the three examples below in both APA and MLA format. Check your work with the style guides.
3. Look up the institutional guidelines for promotion, tenure, or other benefits at your institution. What do they say about receiving credit for reviewing?

References

Belcher, W. (n.d.). *Writing the Academic Book Review.* Retrieved 24 February 2015 from www.wendybelcher.com/pages/documents/WritingtheAcademicBookReview.pdf.

Egbert, J. (2004). Review of *Connected Speech. Language Learning and Technology, 8*(1), 24–28.

Egbert, J. (2010). Review of Evans, M. (Ed.). (2009). *Foreign language learning with digital technology.* London: Continuum International Publishing Group. 224 pp. *The Journal of Educational Research, 103*, pp. 223–225, DOI:10.1080/00220670903530420

Egbert, J., & Sanden, S. (2014). *Foundations of education research: Understanding theoretical components.* Florence, KY: Routledge/Taylor & Francis.

Egbert, J., & Sanden, S. (2015). *Writing education research: Guidelines for publishable scholarship.* Florence, KY: Routledge/Taylor & Francis.

Krauss, L. (2007). *The physics of Star Trek.* New York: Basic Books.

Raschka, C. (2007). *Yo! Yes?* Jefferson City, MO: Scholastic, Inc.

Professional Book Review

Egbert, J. (2010). *The Journal of Educational Research*, 103:223–225.

Evans, M. (Ed.). (2009). *Foreign Language Learning with Digital Technology*. London: Continuum International Publishing Group. 224 pp.

The overall goal of *Foreign Language Learning with Digital Technology* is to explore the relationships between digital technologies and pedagogy through reports of action research. The focus is on "the role of technologies in bringing about frameworks for innovation" (p. xi). Here, innovation does not necessarily lie in the basic way language is thought about and taught but rather in more engagement with language and tasks that are relevant to teachers and learners in the contexts being described. In fact, few of the practical ideas offered seemed different from what can be found throughout the English as a Second Language (ESL) literature. However, the authors explain these ideas within a consistent framework of sound pedagogical principles, provide students more access to language, and make themselves and other teachers more aware of their pedagogy. This focus on pedagogy is one that has long been neglected in the educational technology and computer-assisted language learning (CALL) literatures, and alone makes this text worth reading. In addition, the approach of all the authors is supportive of the use of information and communication technologies (ICT) in education but also appropriately skeptical. The book asks whether technology can transform learning—making it a different thing—or whether it serves merely as another tool for what teachers already do. In this case, it appears that the answer is that it is a tool that can help make learning more efficient for all learners.

The useful aspects of this text are many. For example, subtitles throughout the text make it easy to read, and the language is clear. The focus of several chapters on relatively simple technologies such as interactive white boards (IWBs) and PowerPoint demonstrates the power of effective pedagogy. In addition, the blend of researchers and teachers who serve as authors lives up to the series editor's promise of presenting a range of perspectives. The text also fills a gap in the literature because educators do not often find principled classroom-based research, and this type of research, modeled throughout the text, has great potential to inform administrators and teachers about what is really going on in technology-enhanced language classrooms.

More specifically, Evans's introduction and Chapter 1 provide an excellent rationale for looking at teacher research in a variety of contexts. He efficiently uses the existing research to support and explain the pedagogical assumptions underlying the authors' work in the book and provides background on their teaching settings. While doing so, he points out fallacies under which the CALL and technology education communities have been working and conducting research. He concludes that the teaching methodology, rather than the medium alone, is the crucial factor in learning.

Mitchell's Chapter 2 carries forward this premise, providing steps for authentic text use and reiterating principles of teaching such as the importance of currency in text. He emphasizes the term *teacher fading* (in the United States known as *gradual release of responsibility*) and the centrality of learning strategies and differentiated instruction, both not often connected in ICT texts. His point that the use of the material is more important than the source of the material is made effectively.

Furthermore, the chart on page 81 of Hawkes's Chapter 4 is an excellent guide for active learning. The learning model that she explicates and presents in several tables succinctly and practically presents best practices. In fact, although the chapter supports PowerPoint as a tool for active learning (which might seem contradictory), every aspect of the tasks she describes, from helping students understand learning objectives to learner self-review, is based on the best pedagogical practices from the literature. Moreover, Hawkes's focus on the one-computer, teacher-led classroom is useful and effective, and she acknowledges that there is more to learn and do.

However, there are also minor issues with the text. Some chapters, such as Chapter 2, contain too much untranslated foreign language that takes away from an understanding of the specific tasks or assignments being described. Another issue is the sheer amount of new jargon throughout the text. The glossary in the back of the text helps but does not stop the vocabulary from sometimes getting in the way of understanding. A final, and more serious, issue with this book is the lack of foundational research. In Chapter 4, for example, the author writes that she and her teachers have "come to believe" (p. 98) or "know from experience" (p. 100) ideas about pedagogy that have been explored well in the research, particularly the ties among student engagement, autonomy, and learning. Notions that are central to teacher development, such as situated learning, are also noticeably absent. This oversight leaves the impression that classroom research is not bound to be grounded in previous research, when a literature review is an important part of all systematic inquiry.

What this book proves, in a way, is that technology in itself really does not matter—even language drills, implemented in pedagogically sound ways, can provide engaging avenues to language acquisition. As Evans notes in the conclusion, all the chapters are different in content and even form, which not only makes the book engaging to read but also clearly helps make the book's point about the importance of pedagogy in relation to digital technologies in education.

Although the audience for this text would be relatively new teachers, researchers, and ICT users, the principles of pedagogy that infuse this text serve as a strong reminder for veterans of how educators need to think about teaching and learning with technology.

Trade Book Review

Journal of Adolescent & Adult Literacy, Volume 58, Issue 1, pages 85–88, September 2014
Hollow City: The Second Novel of Miss Peregrine's Peculiar Children
YA Paranormal/Supernatural Fantasy: Ransom Riggs. 2014. Philadelphia: Quirk Books
Reviewed by Will Schmieding, College of Charleston, Charleston, SC, USA. (Schmieding, 2014)

Hollow City, the sequel to *Miss Peregrine's Home for Peculiar Children*, picks up the story immediately when and where the first book ends—in 1940 off the coast of England. Jacob Portman and his newfound, peculiar friends, having lost their home on Cairnholm Island, embark on a time-traveling adventure to war-ridden London to save Miss Peregrine. In this second novel of Miss Peregrine's Peculiar Children, Ransom Riggs continues his fantastic story accompanied by bizarre photographs that keep readers on the edge of their seats.

While all of Miss Peregrine's Peculiar Children certainly develop a great deal as characters in this novel, Jacob discovers that he is not so normal after all. Jacob becomes more familiar with his own peculiarity as the novel progresses, which makes him realize that he is more like his late Grandpa Portman than he could have ever imagined. With the help of a band of gypsies, a peculiar boxer dog, and many other uncanny characters, Jacob and the party of peculiar folk face many strange and intimidating obstacles on their journey.

Using clues from a book of children's *Peculiar Tales* to guide them, along with Jacob's peculiar ability to keep them safe, the group crosses through many exotic loops on their quest. They face hollows, wights, Nazis, and normals on their mission to save their headmistress, Miss Peregrine, from being trapped in her bird state forever. To Jacob and the peculiar children's surprise, the entire peculiardom is in danger!

Hollow City has an energetic plotline that makes the book difficult to set down. Ransom Riggs introduces some new, abominable characters and situations that will send chills down the reader's spine. Keeping in the spirit of the first novel, the photographs in *Hollow City* are equally disturbing and opportunely placed throughout the story. Fans of *Miss Peregrine's Home for Peculiar Children* will certainly be enthralled by the sequel. I would recommend this book to any reader who enjoys paranormal fiction, with a dose of time travel. *Hollow City* will be an enjoyable read for middle school age youth all the way up to adults. Ransom Riggs delivers the goods with his second novel, and all readers will be anticipating more of his works to hit the shelves.

Media Review

Reviewed by Joy Egbert, Washington State University

Overview of Pronunciation in Language Learning

To be able to speak and listen in a second language, it is clear that language learners need something other than just phonemic correctness. As or more important seems to be the ability to comprehend and produce in a near-native-like fashion aspects of pronunciation such as stress, intonation, rhythm, and pacing, and to use gestures and body language appropriately; in other words, to have both linguistic and sociolinguistic competence (Celce-Murcia, Brinton, & Goodwin, 1996; Florez, 1999). In many cases, however, pronunciation teaching still focuses on discrete phonemic awareness and production. For many reasons, this approach has been relatively ineffective to date (Boku, 1998; Donahue, 1999). Fraser (1999) notes that most language learners feel that pronunciation is a crucial part of language learning. Students believe the best way to improve their pronunciation is to practice, and many pronunciation experts agree that pronunciation teaching and learning must be situated in communicative contexts (Fraser, 1999; Levis, 1999; Otlowski, 1998; Wennerstrom, 1999) and help students to use metacognitive strategies in broader communication (Vitanova & Miller, 2002). Otlowski and Fraser (1999) concur with much of the current research that the goals of pronunciation teaching should be "developing functional intelligibility, communicability, increased self-confidence, the development of speech monitoring abilities and speech modification strategies for use beyond the classroom" (p. 3).

In order to reach these goals, Morley (1991) and Fraser (1999) call for more emphasis on individual learners' needs, supporting a learner-centered approach that involves authentic tasks and the use of peers and groups for interaction and feedback to help learners be critical listeners and develop the ability to notice and repair their own and others' errors. In this model, the role of the teacher is facilitator rather than error corrector or ultimate speech model. In the facilitator role, the teacher can offer various models, provide opportunities for practice, suggest specific techniques, and give encouragement and advice to learners as they work toward intelligibility. Morley (1991) calls this role the "speech coach." Fraser (2000) calls for "high quality, effective materials, especially computer-based materials with audio demonstrations, for learners of ESL pronunciation" (p. 2). Such materials, according to Chun (1998), would have to "present authentic speech samples within their cultural contexts and call learners' attention" (p. 73) to specific features. She also suggests that the software must support pair interaction and emphasize natural discourse.

Features of Protea's Connected Speech

Connected Speech is in many ways built on the theoretical foundation outlined above. The manual that accompanies Connected Speech (CS) states that the goal of the software is to improve clarity and accuracy of spoken communication and to help students develop effective communication skills. CS claims to do so by helping learners to identify suprasegmental features of spoken English, to reproduce them, and to be able to evaluate whether they did it well. The software, described explicitly in Darhower (2002), covers pause groups, pitch change, word and syllable stress, and linked words, and also has exercises in minimal pairs and syllable recognition. CS uses speech recognition to evaluate whether learners have produced sounds "acceptably." CS's approach is defined as "meaningful context" in which video plays a central role. CS is theme based, incorporating video speeches on topics ranging from "butterflies as pets" to "running a marathon." According to the program's documentation, the activities are "interactive." Among other advantages, CS says that it provides opportunities for learners to control pace, choose authentic aspects, and receive help and feedback. Darhower (2002) documents technical problems with the software that might frustrate learners (and instructors), typically with the voice recording segments of the program.

Evaluating Software in Pronunciation Teaching and Learning

In order to evaluate pronunciation software, we need to assess how well it teaches, or helps us to teach, in ways that will help students improve their pronunciation. This review is based on seven criteria taken from the literature described above. This list is not all-inclusive, nor does its use imply that the software must meet all of these conditions. These focused criteria, however, can serve as a basis for a discussion of the effectiveness of a software package for pronunciation teaching and learning.

Evaluation

1. Present Authentic Speech Samples and Natural Discourse

In CS, nine people with different North American regional accents and ways of speaking provide stories and information to the learner in each of three levels. The learner can listen to a brief greeting from each character to get an idea of what that person sounds like. The learner works extensively with the short audio presentation from the character. Although the documentation claims that the speech samples are unscripted, the speech sounds unnaturally fluent and slow. Even in Level 3 recordings, word endings are very well pronounced, and the speech is stilted-sounding to a native speaker. In fact, the character Guillermo spoke so slowly and clearly that it was very difficult to determine links and pitch even in Level 1 exercises. His speech, however, was very easy to comprehend and this might assist learners to develop listening skills. In addition, because there is no interaction among characters in the videos (they are the ubiquitous "talking heads"), there is no chance to listen to natural discourse in this program. The characters exhibit few sociolinguistic clues, even little facial expression, to aid in comprehension and the learning of these skills. To fill this gap, the instructor can develop communication tasks for students centered on the themes and exercises in the program; for example, they might work in pairs with Web-based materials to determine what kind of butterfly would make the best pet.

2. Focus Learners' Attention on Both Segmental and Suprasegmental Features

This is a real strength of CS. It is very complete and thorough and provides many opportunities for learners to work explicitly with both kinds of features. Learners can listen, produce, and learn about these features through a large number of exercises on any of three levels.

3. Support Social Interaction and Communication

While the ultimate goal of CS is to improve students' oral communication, there are no opportunities within the software itself for authentic communication and no real examples of such. According to the documentation, CS is intended for independent or school use, as a supplement to classroom instruction, or for pairs in cooperative groups. CS does not support social interaction between learners per se. However, instructors could supplement with activities to support discussion about topics such as how "native" speakers sound different from each other or whether anyone would like to have a butterfly for a pet. Instructors could also assign roles to learners working in dyads to ensure that each learner has a reason to focus and work during program use.

4. Focus on Intelligibility

The speech recognition features of CS provide opportunities for learners to test whether their language is intelligible, but there are several problems with this feature. First, as Darhower (2002) found, the speech recognition does not always work, and when it does it does not always work well. In addition, whether the computer can recognize an utterance might not have any relation to whether the same utterance can be recognized by other speakers. Finally, this feature can recognize intonation, stress, and other suprasegmental features of language, but it cannot determine whether the sentence is grammatical or semantically plausible. These limitations are consistent across software programs that use speech recognition in its current state; instructors might want to prepare students ahead of time to work within these restrictions.

5. Support the Development of Metacognition and Critical Listening

According to pronunciation research, this happens through real communication, which is not possible with CS. Perhaps future research with this software will demonstrate that learners can develop these skills through its use.

6. Provide Opportunities for Practice

CS does provide many opportunities for practice with both segmental and suprasegmental features. This practice is within the context of the audio clips, but because of the limitations of the technology, it is typically drill-based. Learners are generally attempting to get closer to the native models presented in the software rather than being judged on whether their communication would be successful during social conversation.

7. Provide Scaffolding and Individualized Feedback

CS provides a variety of scaffolds for learners. For example, help is present in the form of both oral and written instructions. In addition, navigation ease provides support for efficient program use, and the consistent interface makes the program easy to use (once learners understand what each icon means). Learners can also replay and/or review all audio and text when the program is in learning mode. Furthermore, written scripts accompany the video segments; however, the script text does not always scroll at the same speed as the audio, and the character's mouth in the video is often slightly behind the audio. The hotwords within the script are useful for learners to understand the clip, but the explanations vary in ease; for example, "to remember" is defined as to "have a picture in mind," which might be equally difficult for learners to understand.

Although these scaffolds are a strength, one major weakness of this software program is the "wrong, try again" approach. Answers are judged either to be correct or incorrect (including some cases where there can be alternate answers) with little other feedback, and answers are supplied after the third attempt with little explanation. Additional explanation would help learners to focus on their specific errors, and the addition of hints after the first and second attempts would support learners in thinking about their answers. For example, when learners are working on determining the number of spoken syllables in words, it might be more effective for some learners to be shown an answer instead of just being told "well done." The teacher (as speech coach) can work with the learners as they use the software to supply some of this important feedback.

Conclusions

CS has strengths and weaknesses. In addition to those listed above, strengths include

- The different versions (North American, Australian, and British English) and the inclusion of a variety of speakers in CS clearly demonstrate to learners that "English" is many different things.
- CS provides a great deal of practice for students who learn well deductively.
- Used by teachers in a focused and well-planned way, CS can benefit learners by providing immediate feedback that learners might not otherwise receive in the classroom.
- The use of CS might be seen as very authentic to some students to whom good pronunciation is important.
- For teachers who are not educated in pronunciation or not confident about their own (which Fraser, 1999, 2000, notes is widespread), CS provides support and help.

On the other hand,

- Learners who do not learn well through drill and repetition might be bored quickly.
  o Many places on the Internet have free pronunciation lessons. Learners can take dictation, listen and repeat, and perform many of the tasks that CS presents.
  o The use of audio e-mail software programs and structured audio chat allows learners not only to participate in real communication but also to understand how intelligible their spoken language is.

- CS requires a lot of teacher guidance to use it to its best advantage.
  - o Learners, especially at the low intermediate level (Level 1), might be overwhelmed with the great number of different features to work on in CS.
- Teachers still need to provide opportunities for real practice.

Taking these comments into consideration, whether or not teachers and learners should use CS depends on programmatic goals, resources, and learner needs.

5

ARRANGING COLLABORATIVE ACTION RESEARCH

Excerpt from Tehama County Department of Education action research project:

> Question: "What reading comprehension test taking strategies will improve my reading comprehension scores to a baseline average of 75 percent?"
>
> (www.tehamaschools.org/department/btsa/
> action-research-samples)

Overview

In this chapter, we take service in a less traditional direction. Specifically, we propose that university faculty include collaborative action research as one option for their service agenda.

Typically, collaborative research is noted under the area of scholarship; we consider that an obvious and appropriate placement. However, we also think that collaborations around action research can simultaneously have elements of service. These collaborations might result in a presentation (Chapter 2) or support of doctoral students (Chapter 7) and, in either situation, add to the knowledge base for the educational community. They might also serve to inform teaching paths for classroom teachers or programmatic directions for teacher education programs. These areas fall under service as defined in this book. Like other service options, action research collaborations hold possibilities for informing the field and affording professional benefits for a faculty member. The real power and unique contribution of collaborative action research lies in its potential to simultaneously contribute across teaching, research, and service.

This chapter addresses:

- Defining action research
- Guidelines for action research
- Responsibilities of collaborators
- The roles of technology in action research
- Listing collaborations on a CV or résumé

Defining Action Research

Overall, "research is a process of discovering essential questions, gathering data, and analyzing it to answer those questions" (Shagoury & Power, 2012, p. 2). As defined by Winter and Munn-Ginnings (2001), "action research is the study of a social situation carried out by those involved in that situation in order to improve both their practice and the quality of their understanding" (pp. 21–22). Action research comes with the advantage of being a well-established form of scientific inquiry with unique attributes that make it particularly suited for the challenges and concerns that practitioners and researchers encounter. These attributes include, for example, its possibility for collaboration; the connections it allows across theory, research, and practice; an appreciation for local knowledge and an insider's perspective; its combined attention to a problem situated in a specific context and a possible solution for it; and its ability to promote practice-oriented accountability (Acosta & Goltz, 2014). In the end, action research distinguishes itself from other empirical options as a tool to influence change (Koshy, Koshy, & Waterman, 2011).

The following scenario shows how these attributes of action research apply in actual use:

A group of math teachers collaborated with university researchers to understand action research and apply it to questions that arose in their classrooms. One teacher explored students' use and responses to a new math text the district was considering for adoption. She was on the textbook adoption committee and wanted to include students' voices in her final determination about this text. She administered a survey to all students, convened a focus group of randomly selected students, and did follow-up interviews with a subset of this group. She analyzed this information individually and collapsed the data to form an integrated understanding of these students' views. This information was a key component for her response as a selection committee member.

This example typifies the criteria for action research noted by Hien (2009):

1. The teachers' primary role is to teach and any research project must not interfere with or disrupt this commitment;
2. Data collection should not be too demanding on the teacher's time;
3. The methodology must be reliable enough to formulate hypotheses confidently and develop strategies applicable to the classroom situation;

4. The teacher should be committed to the research problem under study;
5. Teachers must follow ethical procedures when carrying out the research; and
6. Classroom research should adopt a perspective where all members of a school community build and share a common vision (p. 97).

Collaborative action research adds other unique and valuable features and benefits. According to Piggot-Irvine (2012), collaboration increases the proximity of decisions for a research project to its location and, as a result, increases the input of those participants who have a vested interest in the project. Collaboration also broadens the expertise available and, ultimately, provides a political lever for policy implementation and change. Fletcher et al. (2008) add the following benefits: public testing of privately held ideas and assumptions, the reduction of self-limiting reflection, an increase of ownership and commitment to a project's findings and suggestions for change, and an increase in the level of change initiatives and receptivity to them.

Action research, whether published or not, is expected by the education field to follow rigorous standards. Winter (1996) offers the following six principles that can help educators evaluate their action research processes and outcomes:

1. Reflexive critique, which is the process of becoming aware of our own perceptual biases;
2. Dialectic critique, which is a way of understanding relationships between the elements that make up various phenomena in our context;
3. Collaboration, which is intended to mean that everyone's view is taken as a contribution to understanding the situation;

4. Risking disturbance, which is an understanding of our own taken-for-granted processes and willingness to submit them to critique;

5. Creating plural structures, which involves developing various accounts and critiques, rather than a single authoritative interpretation;

6. Theory and practice internalized, which is seeing theory and practice as two interdependent yet complementary phases of the change process (p. 13).

These principles do not explain how to collect and analyze data nor other details linked to this research tradition; however, they do set the stage for understanding the important premises that uniquely undergird action research.

Guidelines for Collaborative Action Research

Although not all institutions will give credit toward promotion and tenure for action research collaborations, the attributes outlined earlier support faculty in discovering more about and adding knowledge to contexts for student learning. However, these benefits will only accrue if the collaboration and research are effectively implemented. The guidelines in this section provide a starting point for those who wish to collaborate.

Decide on a question. As general guidelines, Hubbard and Power (1999) pose several suggestions for creating questions for action research. First, faculty and/or teachers should start with a question of importance within the context of their work and for which they genuinely seek insight, and they should avoid questions that require a yes or no response. Second, they should use language that is easily understood rather than filled with jargon and avoid value-laden words or phrases. Following are sample questions posed by Hubbard and Power:

- How does modeling of the questioning stage of the peer-review process affect the way students question their classmates' writing?
- What happens when a government class bases its curriculum on students' concerns?
- What happens when students identified with special needs engage in discussions during reading time?
- How does the use of storytelling help students learn historical information?

Choose a context for a collaborative action research project. Selecting a context for collaborative research includes working out the participants and the site and naturally stems from the participants and the questions they hold. Because action research is participant initiated, their contexts are typically suitable for the questions under consideration. In other words, the site is obvious, and access to it should be readily attainable.

Create a plan. Collaborative action research projects benefit from a well-organized schedule. A schedule does more than keep a research project moving forward; it also further identifies who is responsible for each event along the way. Answering questions around *why, who, what, when,* and *where* provides an organizational starting point:

- Responding to *why* requires a specification of the question(s) to be addressed and the rationale behind them.
- Knowing *whom* the research includes establishes the people involved beyond the investigators and alerts them to the permissions needed for the project.
- Determining *what* speaks to data collection and analysis.
- Identifying *when* sets a time schedule.
- *Where* further delineates the places of the various research events.

In this process, first the investigators settle on the research question (e.g., What reading strategies best position students to better comprehend a literary text?) and any subquestions linked to it (e.g., How did the teachers implement these strategies? How did students respond to the various strategies?). In deciding who would be involved, the team notes that collaborative research projects can occur between faculty and school staff, two or more professors, or even a professor and undergraduate students within the context of an education course. If part of a course assignment, this type of collaboration adds a need to have learning outcomes that link to the course's expectations. An attention to assessment in order to determine a course grade adds yet another dimension to this collaborative experience that does not need attention in other collaborative contexts. To determine where the project would be implemented, the team explores whether to conduct this project in several classes or to initially select one class. If settling on one class, they would then need to determine selection criteria for the specific class. If required, they would next prepare assent (i.e., permission) forms for their students and, since the students are not 18, obtain consent forms for their parents or guardians. They would then move to selecting the products and assessments that would allow them to better understand their research questions. They know they want comprehension measures but need to decide whether to include formative and summative products and/or formal and standardized measures. They settle on a combination of assessments and then move on to select an appropriate tool for the standardized measure and to determine who will create the formative and summative assessments. They then establish dates for each of these steps and end with determining the locations for instruction and assessment and a central location for the standardized measure.

As the action research collaborators move across the process, they hold in mind that they are engaging in action research and address the rigorous standards that help make their solutions to the initial problem valid and reliable. Suggestions from the American Educational Research Association (AERA, 2015) might prove helpful:

- development of a logical, evidence-based chain of reasoning;
- methods appropriate to the questions posed;
- observational or experimental designs and instruments that provide reliable and generalizable findings;
- data and analysis adequate to support findings;
- explication of procedures and results clearly and in detail, including specification of the population to which the findings can be generalized.

Optional to this process are these additional recommendations:

- adherence to professional norms of peer review;
- dissemination of findings to contribute to scientific knowledge; and
- access to data for reanalysis, replication, and the opportunity to build on findings. (www.aera.net/Publications/StandardsforResearchConduct)

Complete action research protections. A consideration of protections necessarily begins with a review by an Institutional Review Board (IRB). Research conducted by a graduate student or faculty member cannot typically proceed without final approval from the IRB and/or the school district. Of paramount concern is a consideration of the participants and making sure that the appropriate measures are in place to maximize a beneficial outcome from their participation and minimize any harm that might occur. The nature of action research often lends itself to an exempt status, defined as research that does not fall under regulatory guidelines created to protect research participants. The following exempt category is the one that most often applies: Research that occurs in established educational settings and involves normal educational practices. This might include research on instructional strategies or a comparison of their effectiveness. It is commonly understood and expected that the research team will take steps to not noticeably single out students during the course of the project and to consistently monitor students' responsiveness to the selected strategies. This "do no harm" expectation means paying close attention to confidentiality by not using students' real names in any data or publication and by keeping the data secured and available only to the researchers. To further attend to confidentiality, they also refrained from discussing the particulars of their work and the students involved in it during the course of the project.

The researchers then hold in mind the six premises for action research, the need for a clear plan, and a delineation of responsibilities to move ahead with data collection and analysis choices. The two scenarios in Figure 5.1 demonstrate how these guidelines might be implemented.

Figure 5.1   Action research scenarios.

Chad is a high school English teacher. He cares deeply about his discipline and the responsibilities of English teachers to help their students read better. He does not see English teachers as reading teachers but rather as teachers of various forms of literature whose students often have difficulty negotiating the text before them. Action research, with its emphasis on local questions of importance and the use of research by a person within that environment to answer them, perfectly suits Chad's interests. Therefore, he receives support

Figure 5.1 (Continued)

from his English teacher colleagues, who agree to join him in exploring the selection and use of research-based literacy practices that assist students' comprehension of literary texts. Because Chad is also a doctoral student at a local university, his advisor, also a former English teacher, collaborates with his team to design and implement the action research project. Once it is completed, Chad and his colleagues have selected and employed a range of literature and collected data that supports its influence on students' comprehension. Chad, as the leader at every stage of this project, presents its process and products at a national conference. His advisor, whose contributions he acknowledges during the presentation, is an audience member.

Mandy and Kate are elementary teachers. Both teach classes that include first- and second-grade students. Students' self-selected and independent reading is a mainstay of their everyday practices. However, they question whether sufficient empirical support exists for this emphasis. They bring their question to a professor at a local university with whom they have enjoyed a long professional relationship. Collaboratively, they agree to engage in an action research project to systematically look at this practice. Their mutual interest in this question sets the stage for their joint consideration of it. They settle on their individual roles within this project, determine the data that will provide insight into their question, and establish a timeline for its various stages. Their genuine interest in this question establishes a commitment to objectivity and the insights that it will unveil. At the conclusion of their work, they find converging support for this practice, which Mandy and Kate confidently continue to employ. These three collaborators then share their findings with colleagues from around the state at a highly regarded regional conference.

The above examples demonstrate some of the attributes of collaborative action research. In both examples, the projects directly inform the teachers' actions in their local context. As university faculty joined the teachers' efforts as consultants or participants, the experiences and knowledge base that could be applied to the project expanded. Finally, disseminating the projects' findings might help to direct educational change. Additional action research projects can be found across the World Wide Web; see, for example, University of Maryland's *Action Research Examples in Education* at www.drawntoscience.org/educators/action-research/action-research-examples.html.

Collaborative action research, in other words, can promote shifts in approaches to learning and programs and provides professional development for a range of stakeholders. One important caveat should be mentioned: the danger exists for the researchers to become overly absorbed by or into the project and the student participants and lose their investigative and necessary dispassionate stance. This is a fine line the researchers must successfully navigate (Arnold, Price, & Moisio, 2006).

Responsibilities of Collaborators

Collaborators in an action research project are first and foremost researchers. Therefore, their shared responsibilities involve expectations for anyone who conducts research. An attention to the ethics of conducting research assumes paramount importance. AERA provides a highly regarded starting point for a broad range of ethical considerations at www.aera.net/AboutAERA/KeyPrograms/SocialJustice/ResearchEthics/tabid/10957/Default.aspx. While all the points matter, the following categories in the AERA list apply especially to collaborations: professional competence; integrity; fabrication, falsification, and plagiarism; avoiding harm; nondiscrimination; nonexploitation; teaching, training, and administering education programs;

authorship credit; dual relationships; informed consent; confidentiality; and use and misuse of expertise. However, not all interactions between researchers count as collaborations. When a true collaboration evolves, several expectations arise. Clearly identifying and then communicating these expectations can prevent the development of future challenges. The Administrators and the Responsible Conduct of Research organization (2015) proposes that future collaborators consider the following questions: What am I expected to contribute to this joint research project? What do I expect to get out of this collaboration? Answering these questions can make for a smooth road as the project progresses. For example, in the scenarios in Figure 5.1, Chad's teaching colleagues and professor understood his lead role and what it entailed. Therefore, when he made a solo presentation of this work, they were neither surprised nor concerned.

Across these various collaborative arrangements, the strength and quality of the collaboration must be nurtured. Piggot-Irvine (2012) proposes a five-level process:

1. Devote time initially to introductions. This might seem unnecessary since collaborative projects typically begin with people who know each other, but remember that knowing people in one context does not mean you know them as collaborators across the many aspects for an action research project. Getting to know each other within this research context matters.

2. Recognize the potential of various members of the research team. This needs to remain an ongoing process so each person continues to feel valued and important individually and as a member of the team.

3. Develop and encourage members to hold an inquiring mindset. Gaining an inquiry perspective goes beyond seeking answers to questions. In collaborations, an inquiry perspective

involves increasing a regard for the perspectives and interpretations of another person's stance.

4. Transition to collaboration, the next level within this model. This becomes possible when the first three conditions are met.

5. Commit to the cogeneration of information a fruitful collaborative action research project requires.

Collaborative action research joins together real people who collectively examine real-life experiences in the social world of education. This opportunity to uncover and support real improvements within educational contexts can serve both the profession and the individual (Zuber-Skerritt, 2012).

The Roles of Technology in Action Research

Technology can assist at various stages of action research. If done collaboratively, it can assist with finding meeting times, keeping track of revisions, and finding additional research. For example, Google Docs and Calendar allow multiple users to view and input information. In addition, as the research proceeds, various software packages can support data collection and analysis (e.g., SPSS for quantitative analysis and Ethnograph for qualitative data). Further, communications software such as e-mail, text, or chat can help researchers keep in touch and up to date.

Listing Collaborations on a CV or Résumé

Depending on who is involved and their reasons for involvement, collaborations can lead to a specific product such as a presentation or a publication, which would then be noted on the vita under the headings for those areas. However, depending on the faculty member's goals and the professional position envisioned, a separate listing of relevant collaborative projects

Figure 5.2 Example vita entries.

Collaborations

2014 Participant

Understanding the Academic Needs of Second Language Learners in a Middle School Science Class
Collaborative action research project with Juan Parker, Teacher, Mesa School District, Mesa, AZ

State and Regional Teacher Research Projects

2013 Lead researcher

Designing and Implementing a STEM Curriculum in an Elementary School Program
State Superintendent of Public Instruction, the Chesterfield School District, and State University

might be deemed appropriate. If so, then collaborators can maintain the format for the vita and add a section to it. Following the format for the other sections of the résumé remains important. In the absence of direction from APA and MLA, the examples in Figure 5.2 might be followed or adapted.

Conclusion

Today's educational arena faces many challenges. Snowden (2010) asserts that action research is well poised as an appropriate methodology for addressing these issues. Further, working in harmony with other stakeholders, which collaborative action research entails, expands the perspectives brought to bear on these issues, and obtaining multiple perspectives also finds support in today's scholarship (e.g., Jordan, Kleinsassser, & Roe, 2014). Meaningful collaboration around a suitable method, therefore, further maximizes the potential to positively impact these "wicked" problems in education. To this end, professional service is both timely and important. As Dick (2012) states,

> Turbulent situations also demand other qualities that action learning and action research can provide. Strong participation generates commitment to collective action. A rigorous attitude to evidence and subsequent sense making can temper the inadequate decisions or rash action that might otherwise take place.
>
> (p. 41)

The various sections of this chapter provide a base for getting started, moving forward, and noting accomplishments in collaborative action research, and therefore, movement toward solutions.

Recommended Resources

- AERA Teacher as Researcher SIG. *Research connections*. Available at www.aera.net/SIG126/TeacherasResearcherSIG126/tabid/11980/Default.aspx.

This site, devoted exclusively to teacher as researcher, contains a wealth of information about journals to consult and communities to join.

- Mills, G. E. (2000). *Action research: A guide for the teacher researcher*. Upper Saddle River, NJ: Prentice-Hall.

This text provides straightforward guidance for conducting action research and is especially applicable for a novice.

- Stringer, E. (20013). *Action research*. Thousand Oaks, CA: Sage.

The many examples noted in this text make it especially helpful for practitioners who are beginning their use of action research.

- Thoms, P., McMasters, R., Roberts, M. R., & Dombkowski, D. A. (1999). Résumé characteristics as predictors of an invitation to interview. *Journal of Business and Psychology, 13*(3), 339–356.

This article provides empirical evidence to guide the construction of a well-received résumé.

- Whyte, W. F. E. (1991). *Participatory action research*. Thousand Oaks, CA: Sage.
  This text focuses exclusively on the inclusion of practitioners in the research process.

Guided Practice

1. Draft a question to shape an area you have wondered about for some time. Return to the suggestions for writing good questions and revise it to have its presentation coincide with those recommendations. Then brainstorm a list of colleagues whom you think might join you to explore this question. Once you establish the group, work together to apply the guidelines for collaborative action research.
2. After reading this chapter, list what you consider the advantages and drawbacks of collaborative action research. Return to this chapter to attend more closely to the areas that apply to them.
3. Revisit your vita and, based on the suggestions in this chapter, revise it to make a place for collaborative action research projects.

References

Acosta, S., & Goltz, H. H. (2014). Transforming practices: A primer on action research. *Health Promotion Practice, 18*(4), 465–470.

Administrators and the Responsible Conduct of Research organization. (2015). *Collaborators' expectations*. Retrieved 22 August 2015 from https://ori.hhs.gov/education/products/rcradmin/topics/colscience/tutorial_4.shtml

American Educational Research Association. (2015). *Research ethics*. Retrieved 22 August 2015 from www.aera.net/AboutAERA/KeyPrograms/SocialJustice/ResearchEthics/tabid/10957/Default.aspx

Arnold, E., Price, L., & Moisio, R. (2006). Making contexts matter: Selecting research contexts for theoretical insights. In R. W. Belk (Ed.), *Handbook of qualitative research methods in marketing* (pp. 106–125). Northampton, MA: Edward Elgar Publishing.

Dick, B. (2012). Action research and action learning for an uncertain and turbulent world. In O. Zuber-Skerritt (Ed.), *Action research for sustainable development in a turbulent world* (pp. 29–44). Bingley, England: Emerald Group Publishing.

Fletcher, M. A., Zuber-Skerritt, O. D., Piggot-Irvine, E., & Bartlett, B. J. (2008). *Qualitative research methods for evaluating action research.* Retrieved from www.nzcer.org.nz/nzcerpress/evaluating-action-research.

Hien, T.T.T. (2009). Why is action research suitable for education? *VNU Journal of Science, Foreign Languages, 25*(2), 97–106.

Hubbard, R. S., & Power, B. M. (1999). *Living the questions: A guide for teacher researchers.* Portland, ME: Stenhouse Publishers.

Jordan, M., Kleinsasser, R., & Roe, M. F. (2014). Wicked problems: Inescapable wickedity. *Journal of Education for Teaching, 40*(4), 415–130.

Koshy, E., Koshy, V., & Waterman, H. (2011). *Action research in healthcare.* London, England: Sage.

Piggot-Irvine, E. (2012). Creating authentic collaboration: A central feature of effectiveness. In O. Zuber-Skerritt (Ed.), *Action research for sustainable development in a turbulent world* (pp. 89–106). Bingley, England: Emerald Group Publishing

Shagoury, R., & Power, B. M. (2012). *Living the questions: A guide for teacher-researchers.* Portland, ME: Stenhouse Publishers.

Snowden, D. (2010). *Narrative research.* Retrieved 10 July 2015 from http://narrate.typepad.com/files/100816-narrative-research_snowden-final.pdf

Winter, R. (1996). Some principles and procedures for the conduct of action research. *New Directions in Action Research.* In O. Zuker-Skerritt (Ed.), *New directions in action research* (pp. 13–27). Washington, DC: Falmer Press.

Winter, R., & Munn-Giddings, C. (2001). *Handbook for action research in health and social care.* London, England: Routledge.

Zuber-Skerritt, O. (Ed.). (2012). *Action research for sustainable development in a turbulent world.* Bingley, England: Emerald Group Publishing.

6

ADMINISTRATIVE SERVICE

Descriptions of committee work:

Committee on Global Diversity
Charge: To promote diversity via developing quality teaching and professional education practices with a goal to promote equity, diversity, and global orientations for educators and their responsiveness to the students whom they serve.

Committee on Innovation and Technology
Charge: To develop the Association's classroom reform and technology agendas as it relates to K–12 and postsecondary education. The Committee should promote the use of innovative strategies and technological interventions in schools and professional education preparation contexts through gathering information about resources and uses, providing leadership related to professional preparation,

facilitating communication and interaction about innovations in learning and technology among faculty in SCDEs, through the dissemination of proven methods and processes in professional education.

American Association of Colleges for Teacher Education

(http://aacte.org/about-aacte)

Overview

This chapter explores service to both education institutions and professional organizations. While serving on editorial boards also provides professional service (as addressed in Chapter 3), this chapter explores participation in an organization's administrative structures. As the quoted selections indicate, a range of possibilities exist depending on the association's mission and its enactment of it. In general, the options include numerous offices and committees.

This chapter addresses:

- Guidelines for administrative and committee roles
- Process and benefits of administrative service
- Responsibilities of official and committee roles
- The roles of technology in administrative and committee work
- Listing professional service on a résumé or vita

Guidelines for Administrative and Committee Roles

Faculty, students, and staff all serve in different ways, but all typically have opportunities to serve in administrative positions on committees and in organizations that serve education in some way. Institutional committees can range from faculty senate to the departmental safety committee, while professional organizations offer volunteer positions from president to awards committee member. The guidelines that follow provide suggestions for how to go about serving in this way.

Choosing Professional Service Options

In higher education, committee work often comes with a specific position; for example, those who teach elementary education courses might be required to serve on an elementary education committee. In other cases, institutions might require service on a set number of committees the faculty or staff member can choose. In growing numbers, graduate students are encouraged to start their service to professional organizations in their field as early as possible. When options to choose types of administrative service do exist, several guidelines can assist in the selection of professional service. They include:

• As noted in previous chapters, base any service on personal interests. Having service goals that coincide with your talents and interests can further help you choose among a myriad of options and combine them into a cohesive whole.
• Identify the organizations most closely aligned with your teaching and research emphasis areas (or, if staff, areas of employment and interest).
• Carefully consider the time available for the level of professional service you consider.
• Weigh the benefits that accrue from professional service.

Using a joint consideration of your interests, time availability, and benefits can then serve as a filter to explore relevant officer and committee opportunities by searching web pages, talking with peers, and/or attending meetings.

Getting Started

As stated previously, getting started in administrative service must begin with the self-reflection necessary to determine service goals in conjunction with a person's interests, talents, and time availability. Once this initial and important task is completed, a selection of appropriate organizations can ensue.

Discover

For some people, the multifaceted nature of their interests and goals leads them to select several organizations they have been referred to by colleagues. For example, a faculty member's teaching and research might overlap around mathematics and teacher education, another's might include literacy and teacher education, while a third might focus on second-language learners and teacher education. In these instances, all might select to explore participation in the American Association of Colleges for Teacher Education (AACTE) and then a second organization unique to their disciplinary interest (e.g., National Council of Teachers of English [NCTM], International Literacy Association [ILA], or Teachers of English to Speakers of Other Languages [TESOL]). These same faculty might also target a specific population such as middle-level students and their teachers and therefore consider the Association of Middle Level Education. A focus on early childhood might lead to the inclusion of the Association for Childhood Education International. A web search or conversation with peers can result in other associations to be considered.

Investigate

A careful perusal of the selected organizations' websites will then allow potential participants to match opportunities with personal preferences and set priorities for where to begin. Simple membership on a committee might be a good place, but again this depends on the time required and on additional issues such as whether travel is necessary. The appendix to this chapter provides sample descriptions of committee positions.

Try It

The rest of the process requires personal initiative and a willingness to take the plunge.

For some opportunities, you will need to complete an application form. These are typically done online with the use of pull-down options and/or relatively short responses. Seeking an elected office might require a written response to an outline of requirements. The requirements typically request a summary of one's educational and work history, the reasons for seeking a specific office, and the vision you hold for the organization and your contributions. Other positions have a more limited request. For example, a call for a webmaster position provided these directions for potential applicants:

> The letter of application should be sent as an email attachment. The letter should address the applicant's previous service to X (if applicable), ability to fulfill the responsibilities listed above, and names of two X organization members who agree to serve as references. The greatest requirement for this office is simply a commitment to X and a willingness to serve.

Figure 6.1 provides a sample letter submitted for this position by a novice in this application process.

Figure 6.1 Sample letter of application for a volunteer service position.

Dear Dr. X,

I am writing this letter as an application for Webmaster of X. I received my Ph.D. in curriculum and instruction with a literacy emphasis in December of 2010 at X University and have a tenure-track position at X. A colleague, (name redacted), showed me this position and I immediately saw an opportunity to serve if you find my background in keeping with your expectations.

I have been involved with web mastering for several years, first as the sole webmaster for X organization across a

Figure 6.1 (Continued)

> two-year period and then in my role as advisor for a local high school paper which went to online availability. As a graduate student, I worked with a science grant with the main objective of keeping the website current for the science collaborative. I was responsible for all the organizing of upcoming conferences on the site and the reporting of past conferences in the state of X for college and career readiness in higher education. I also needed to add materials to keep this site updated.
>
> I am willing to travel to complete any online training needed to keep your website going and giving the up-to-the-minute information to colleagues across the country. I enjoy computer work and would love to be able to help in this capacity if you consider my experiences in keeping with your expectations.
>
> Thanks for your time and consideration. I hope to hear from you soon and be able to serve actively and with pride. As requested in the application notification, the following members of the organization have agreed to serve as references:
>
> Sincerely,
X, Ph.D.
X University
Assistant professor, Curriculum and Instruction

As you write a letter for the first time, make sure to address each request noted in the application explanation. In addition, as done in the letter in Figure 6.1, include each bit of experience that applies.

Benefit

The process ends with a sense of accomplishment stemming from your collaborative and collegial professional service. As Edwards,

McMillon, and Turner (2010) state, "Together we can be victorious" (p. 164).

Process and Benefits of Administrative Service

Professional service places you as a contributor to an organization's attainments. As an additional incentive, professional service also comes with the expansion of professional contacts noted in the following hypothetical examples of Brad, Stephanie, and Jocelyn.

Brad's Professional Service Journey

As a doctoral student, Brad began professional service by reviewing manuscripts for a local publication offered by his college. He also began presenting at a conference linked to his research orientations. In addition, as a new assistant professor, he volunteered to review conference proposals for the organization, where he had a history of presenting. This role, then, offered an appropriate first step for his professional service as an academic. After establishing a track record as a proposal reviewer, he then volunteered to serve on the editorial board for this organization and was also selected. Since this organization has a publication committee, he deemed his membership on it in keeping with his service record for the organization and his interest. When a call went out seeking applicants for this committee, he submitted his name. Because of his previous experience, he was selected. He then went on to eventually chair this committee. This sequence of participation allowed him to move membership experiences to a leadership role, which further enriched and broadened his professional service accomplishments. They also placed him in a position to more closely interact with senior faculty who participated in this organization's leadership. Making these acquaintances provided the benefits of expanding his professional network and further building his readiness for a broadening of his service participation. In this case, he was encouraged to run for the organization's Board of Directors. While not selected for the ballot the first time he applied for this appointment, he was encouraged to try again. His willingness to resubmit his name was rewarded by making the ballot and being elected as a Board member. During this time, Brad also expanded his service to a second organization and, initially, followed the same basic path: from reviewing conference submissions to receiving a spot on this organization's editorial board. At this point, he decided to volunteer to serve on the awards committee that selected the outstanding master's thesis and doctoral dissertations. Brad continues to consider further possibilities. When his tenure and promotion year arrived, he not only had a nice list of professional service to note but also had met many senior faculty who shared his research interests. He recommended some of them as external reviewers for his promotion and tenure dossier.

Stephanie's Professional Service Journey

Stephanie has an appointment at a university that focuses primarily on teaching. She currently teaches four courses per semester, which places extra importance on selecting professional service wisely and well. She prefers opportunities that afford a specific and bounded time frame rather than a year-long commitment. With these responsibilities and preferences in mind, she carefully looked for options that coincided with them and her interests. She selected an organization that focuses on teacher education, where she regularly attends and typically presents. She began by volunteering to serve as a session chair for this organization's annual conference. This role does not involve any preplanning or additional travel. Being selected gave her the opportunity to complete the duties of the chair (i.e., explaining the collection of papers, introducing the individual presenters, and keeping the presentations and discussion within the allotted time frame) while hearing interesting talks around topics of personal interest. She also volunteered to be a committee member for the selection of an award to honor a member with outstanding service to this organization. This committee's work started in October and ended in November, which offered a time frame that suited her tight schedule. Like Brad, she also extended her professional network, meeting junior faculty, with whom she developed some group projects linked to her teaching agenda, and senior faculty, whose acquaintance served her well as she approached promotion and tenure.

Jocelyn's Professional Service Journey

Jocelyn amassed a strong service record as an undergraduate student and high school math teacher. She mentored math students as an undergraduate and served as an undergraduate representative for a local chapter of an organization for future and current math teachers. As a teacher, she served as an advisor for the local student chapter of this same organization and eventually became president of its state organization. While a doctoral student, she remained busy with her demands as a full-time student and research assistant but still found time to serve as a graduate student representative on search committees and to assist her advisor, who held the role of a conference chair for a major professional organization. As a new assistant professor, she set her sights on continuing a strong service commitment. She began by indicating her interests in various committees and received an invitation to serve on two of them: the membership committee and the rules and regulations committee. When approached about her interest in chairing the membership committee, she agreed and was appointed. As time passed, she ran for an elected office as executive secretary. She won this election and is in her second term in this role.

These examples are unique in the paths taken by Brad, Stephanie, and Jocelyn, but they hold several commonalities. First, all three educators started professional service early. (While this chance might have passed for some readers of this text, the other examples remain feasible.) They built their service on a strong sense of their interests and circumstances, and they were willing to self-nominate and risk rejection (and some experienced it). In addition, they took advantage of service opportunities as a basis for future service. Further, they capitalized on their professional service to appropriately nurture their professional networks. They engaged in these activities willingly and thoughtfully. Their efforts benefitted the professional organizations, their professional growth, and their personal sense of accomplishment.

Responsibilities of Higher Administrative Roles

Every organization holds substantive and subtle differences for its various leadership and committee roles. One thing that many members do not understand is the progression of roles that lead to the presidency of an organization; this is a service role that is held in esteem and earns prestige in higher education. The progression often begins with election as a vice president for year one and then an automatic progression to president-elect and president. Each position is a one-year appointment. Many organizations also extend to past president and past-past president, each role coming with specific responsibilities. The Association of Literacy Educators and Researchers (ALER) affords an example of this progression and related responsibilities. The vice president for ALER is elected by the membership and then charged with oversight for ALER's various committees. The vice president makes sure each committee has a chair (or in some cases co-chairs) in place, that membership numbers coincide with the by-laws, and that the committee's charges are understood and enacted. Vice presidents hold an automatic place as a member of the Board of Directors and the Executive Committee. The president-elect is responsible for every aspect of the annual conference's program and continues to serve on the Board of Directors as well as the Executive Committee. The details of organizing a conference make this an intense and busy year. As president, the responsibilities shift to presiding at all meetings, supervising the many affairs of the organization, and giving a presidential address at the annual conference. Following this three-year stint, the year as past president comes with the responsibility to establish and chair the Awards Committee. The final year, serving as past-past president, involves chairing the Elections Committee, making sure that the slate of officers is complete and that the nominees' biographies are secured and in compliance with the guidelines for them. Holding in mind that the election for what is really one office comes with a five-year obligation is extremely important to understand and to be prepared to fulfill. Again, other organizations might hold different time frames and duties, so carefully perusing the organization's website as well as talking with people who have held these roles can inform a decision to seek this level of involvement and commitment.

The Roles of Technology in Administrative and Committee Work

Technology can serve several purposes in administrative and committee work. For example, the use of the tracking system available in word processing software can assist with the creation of a collaborative document. In addition, e-mail attachments allow for a quick and easy way to share documents. Scheduling applications such as Doodle can ease the burden of finding meeting times, and the use of polling software such as PollEverywhere makes it simple to obtain feedback. Further, many options exist when a need to interact with people across sites exists. These include landline phones for conference calls, the commonly owned and used smartphones, online meeting options that allow face-to-face encounters such as Skype or an interactive broadcast system; these technologies mean that the ability to productively meet and complete a sundry of committee or administrative tasks is no longer hamstrung by distance.

Listing Professional Service on a CV or Résumé

Once you have determined what kind of professional service you want to do and have been selected or elected for it, you want to have your curriculum vita or résumé clearly identify your contributions. Like other items addressed in previous chapters, a specific format for including administrative service does not exist. The big point to remember is that your overall presentation should conform with other sections in terms of font size and use of bold, italics, and underlining. As Perlmutter (2010) underscores,

> The content of a tenure packet is undoubtedly more important than its presentation. But, as in many aspects of life and labor, professionalism in packaging and design counts. The best thing you can do for your tenure packet is to make it as impressive in clarity and organization as in substance.
>
> (p. 165)

A CV or résumé that will become part of that tenure packet deserves comparable attention to format and substance.

Figures 6.2 and 6.3 provide examples that tap service options offered by major professional organizations. They provide formats for you to adopt or adapt to fit your needs and to coincide with the overall format used for other sections.

Figure 6.2 Administrative service entries.

Professional Activities

American Educational Research Association

Proposal Reviewer, 1992, 1996, 2004–2006, 2011

Association of Literacy Educators and Researchers

Past President, 2011–2012
President, 2010–2011
President-Elect, 2009–2010
Vice President, 2008–2009
Board of Directors, 2004–2008
Proposal Reviewer, 1992–present

Association of Middle Level Educators

Research Advisory Committee, 2009–2015
Proposal Reviewer, 1994, 2012

International Literacy Association

Dina Feitelson Award Committee, 2011–2014
Subcommittee on Research Awards, 2011–2012
Elva Knight Research Grant Reviewer, 2012
Proposal Reviewer, 1993–1995, 1995–1997, 1997–1999, 2001–2013
Subcommittee on Outstanding Dissertation of the Year, 2008–2011
Research Awards Subcommittee, 2006–2008
Subcommittee on Special Service Award, 1998–2000

Literacy Research Association

Proposal reviewer, 2008–to date
Field Council, 2011–present
Albert J. Kingston Award Committee, 2003–2005
Student Award Committee, 1999–2000

National Council for Accreditation of Teacher Education

Board of Examiners, 2007–2010

Several features are notable in this example. It has a heading to indicate the content of the section. This example then arranges the entries in alphabetical order by the professional organization. Under each organization, the various positions held are then listed chronologically. Service could also be listed by date rather than organization in order to allow readers to find recent contributions easily.

Another option would involve listing all the entries by type of contribution and using headings such as leadership roles, committees, and proposal and manuscript review boards. The specific information would then be added by organization and look like Figure 6.3.

Figure 6.3 Alternative format for vita entries.

Professional Activities

Leadership roles

> Association of Literacy Educators and Researchers, President, 2014
> Association of Literacy Educators and Researchers, President-elect, 2013
> Association of Literacy Educators and Researchers, Vice President, 2012

Committee membership

> Association of Middle Level Educators, Research Advisory Committee, 2013–present
> International Literacy Association, Elva Knight Research Grant Reviewer, 2012

Proposal reviews

> Literacy Research Association, 1989–present
> American Educational Research Association, 1992, 1996, 2004–2006, 2011

No matter which format is chosen, the focus should be on readability.

Conclusion

Service to the profession can take numerous directions and include a range of activities; selecting them should be done with clearness of purpose and a willingness to devote the time and effort required for accomplishing the chosen task at a high level. One cautionary note remains to be restated: the need to carefully consider costs and benefits, particularly in time spent. Making a distinction between having time to do service and choosing to spend time doing service is an important one. The availability and use of time should be considered in arranging any service schedule—and many faculty benefit from having one. Perlmutter (2010) offers three relevant suggestions for maximizing the use of time and obtaining promotion and tenure: (1) reduce distractions, (2) get e-mail under control, and (3) begin with the big picture—clearly considering what you want to accomplish with teaching, research, and service. Giving too much of yourself to any one part of your job (teaching, research, or service) can result in other parts suffering from neglect. In the end, service can and should play an important role in our professional lives.

Recommended Resources

Consult the website for any professional organization that fits your interests. Following are a range of examples:

American Association of Colleges for Teacher Education: aacte.org
Association for Middle Level Education: amle.org
Association of Childhood Education International: www.acei.org/

> Association of Teacher Educators: www.ate1.org/pubs/
> home.cfm
> National Council for Teachers of Mathematics: nctm.org
> National Council of Teachers of English: ncte.org
> TESOL International Organization: www.tesol.org/

- Greene, H. C., O'Connor, K. A., Good, A. J., Ledford, C. C., Peel, B. B., & Zhang, G. (2008). Building a support system toward tenure: Challenges and needs of tenure-track faculty in colleges of education. *Mentoring & Tutoring: Partnership in Learning, 16*(4), 429–447.

  Serving as an officer or committee member for a professional organization must fit within the obligations for promotion and tenure. This article addresses the merging of these varied obligations.

- Misra, J., Lundquist, J. H., Holmes, E., & Agiomavritis, S. (2011). The ivory ceiling of service work. *Academe, 97*(1), 22–26.

  This article introduces an important cautionary note into a consideration of service—especially for women.

Guided Practice

1. Select one goal for professional service. Determine the steps required to accomplish it and create a timeline for reaching it.
2. Keep a log of your use of time during a typical work day. Examine it to determine how to maximize efficiencies and make room for service.
3. Using the examples from Brad, Stephanie, and Jocelyn, write a scenario that captures your hopes for your professional service trajectory. Revisit it at regular intervals to note your progress.

4. Revisit the letter for a webmaster service opportunity written by an assistant professor. What revisions would you suggest to further strengthen it?

References

Edwards, P. A., McMillon, G. T., & Turner, J. D. (2010). *Change is gonna come: Transforming literacy education for African American students.* New York: Teachers College Press.

Perlmutter, D. D. (2010). *Promotion and tenure confidential.* Cambridge, MA: Harvard University Press.

From the Association of Literacy Educators and Researchers (ALER)

(www.aleronline.org/?page=constitution)

Goals of the Association of Literacy Educators and Researchers:

To stimulate the self-development and professional growth of teachers and reading specialists at all educational levels.

To encourage the continuing improvement of college and university curricula and encourage preparation programs for teachers and reading specialists.

To encourage the continuing improvement of administrative, clinical, diagnostic, and instructional practices related to the learning process.

The President shall:

a) Preside at all meetings of the Association
b) Serve as Chairperson of the Board of Directors

c) Hold membership, ex-officio on all standing Committees other than the Elections Committee
d) Co-sign all contracts and other instruments of the Association
e) Present with the Business Manager/Treasurer and the Executive Secretary the annual budget to the Board of Directors
f) Supervise the affairs of the Association in the implementation of its purposes
g) Present an annual report to the membership at the Legislative Assembly
h) Collaborate with the Executive Secretary and the Vice President to appoint Committees and commissions, designate Chairpersons of all Committees and commissions, and define in writing the duties and responsibilities of the Committees and commissions
i) Discharge and remove any Committee Chairpersons who fail to fulfill their authorized duties or cease to be members of the Association in good standing. In such cases the President shall appoint a successor.

Directors are liaisons to committees and offices that are grouped into three categories: Marketing, Conference, and Operations.

Marketing includes the following: Public Information, Membership, Publications, and Legislative and Social Issues.

Conference includes: Conference Coordinator, Conference Program Chair, Exhibits/Reading Room, Awards, Research, and Photographer.

Operations includes: Professional Affairs, Elections, Resolutions and Rules, and Historian.

From the Literacy Research Association

(www.literacyresearchassociation.org/index.php?option=com_content&view=article&id=89)

Goal of the Association: LRA is a community of current and future scholars dedicated to the dissemination of ethical and socially responsible, rigorous and methodologically diverse research to those who could benefit.

Field Council
Charges

1. The LRA Field Council shall serve as an advisory council to the LRA President and Board of Directors regarding the work of the Literacy Research Association.
2. Every year the Field Council Representatives in each state/province/country should contact faculty at colleges and universities within their assigned areas to encourage the acquisition, renewal, or maintenance of subscriptions to the *LRA Yearbook* and the *Journal of Literacy Research*.
3. Field Council members are encouraged to arrange co-sponsored meetings at state and regional meetings of other literacy organizations with the understanding that LRA does not guarantee program slots at the annual LRA meeting for co-sponsoring organizations. Co-sponsoring organizations are invited to submit program proposals for consideration under the regulations of the LRA Call for Proposals.

Awards Committee: Appointment of Members

The Past President will be responsible for appointing members to the Committees in consultation with the Committee Chair. In order for individuals to be appointed and serve on Committees, they must be members in good standing. The Past President will confirm the members' willingness to serve on the Committee via either written or e-mail confirmation. The appointment of Committee members to Awards Committees shall be announced at the fall Executive Committee meeting. (In a subsequent section, the term of office is noted as a three-year commitment.)

From the American Association of Colleges for Teacher Education

(http://aacte.org/about-aacte)

Goal of the Association: The American Association of Colleges for Teacher Education defines itself as "a national alliance of educator preparation programs dedicated to high-quality, evidence-based preparation that assures educators are ready to teach all learners on Day 1." Its stated vision is to serve as the major voice for educator preparation with a mission to "lead the field in advocating for and building capacity for high-quality educator preparation programs in a dynamic landscape."

Board of Directors

Some of the members of this Board are elected while others are appointed. The responsibilities of this Board include providing guidance for the direction of AACTE by establishing policies. It meets twice per year to fulfil its responsibilities.

Committee on Research and Dissemination

Charge: To develop the Association's research agenda in order to assist the membership to develop research-informed professional consensus regarding professional education in the following areas: standards, curriculum, pedagogy, assessment, accountability, and workforce development. The Committee will also consider effective vehicles and strategies for synthesizing and disseminating research findings as those findings inform the consensus discussion and contribute to the capacity building of the field and member institutions. The Committee will serve as the editorial board for the *Journal of Teacher Education*, and it administers the Association's Writing and Research Awards, issuing an annual call for entries and reviewing applications for the Outstanding Book Award, Outstanding Dissertation Award, and Outstanding

JTE Article Award. The Committee will serve to select Fellowship recipients, provide guidance as appropriate, and to provide feedback on the overall effectiveness of the Fellowship program.

Washington State University

https://faculty.wsu.edu/career/service-opportunities/

Service Opportunities

Faculty Senate Committees

Faculty Senate committees make recommendations to the Faculty Senate for changes in policies and procedures related to their areas of expertise (e.g., academic affairs). They might also report their views to administrators. Members of Senate Committees are elected by the members of the Faculty Senate. Nominations for these committees are made by the Committee on Committees and are taken from the floor. A list of Faculty Senate Committees and more information about these committees might be found at the link above.

Faculty Senate Officers

The Chair of the Faculty Senate presides over meetings of the Senate. To ensure orderly transitions, the Chair is assisted by a Chair Elect and a Past Chair. The Chair Elect is selected by a vote of members of the Faculty Senate. After that, the Chair Elect serves for one year before becoming Chair for one year and then Past Chair for one year. The Faculty Senate Chair receives a 0.5 FTE appointment and the Chair Elect receives a 0.25 FTE appointment. The Executive Secretary of the Faculty Senate joins the three chairs to make up the Faculty Senate Executive Committee which meets regularly with the President and Provost. The Executive Secretary is nominated by the Faculty Senate Executive Committee and is elected by the Faculty

Senate for a 3-year term. The Executive Secretary receives a 0.5 FTE appointment.

Faculty Senate Steering Committee

The Faculty Senate Steering Committee meets on alternate weeks with the Faculty Senate. It is composed of the chairs of major Faculty Senate Committees and the Faculty Senate Officers. The Steering Committee sets the agenda for upcoming meetings of the Faculty Senate and acts on the Senate's behalf during the summer.

Faculty Status Committee

The Faculty Status Committee (FSC) adjudicates disputes among faculty members and between faculty members and the administration (e.g., denials of tenure and/or promotion). Any member of the faculty, including fixed-term (temporary) faculty, might bring a problem to the attention of the Committee. The Committee currently has ten tenured faculty members, each serving for three years. FSC can also designate other members of the faculty to assist in its work. FSC is unique among committees because it solicits nominations from, is elected by, and is responsible to, the faculty. FSC writes reports and makes recommendations to the faculty and to the President. It also periodically reports to the Senate and to the faculty concerning its operations.

Presidential Committees

Presidential committees are appointed by, and responsible to, the President. Unlike some of the Faculty Senate Committees, Presidential committees include representatives from administrative professionals, classified staff and students. Faculty nominees for these committees are recommended by the Faculty Senate's Committee on Committees. A list of Presidential committees and more information about them might be found by clicking on the link above.

7

MENTORING STUDENTS

Comment from advisor to a student:

> You have some interesting ideas here. The issue with publishing is
> that there have to be conclusions for a broader audience either about
> the topic or about the method used to investigate them. If you can
> couch these papers in a larger theoretical framework (something from
> linguistics, probably), you could submit them to a variety of applied
> linguistics journals. It would be a lot of work, but you can do it . . .

Message from a student to advisor:

> Thank you very, very much for your time, comments, and advice. Your
> comments are very valuable and helpful to understand the incon-
> sistency of the paper. I am not deleting your comments from the

document this time so that you can see my response to the comments. I would appreciate your comments on the structure of the paper. Have a very good day and happy weekend.

Overview

In previous chapters we discussed reviewing academic manuscripts and other aspects of professional service that might each play a role in mentoring students. However, obtaining a good understanding of a student's background, abilities, and goals and interacting on a repeated basis is substantively different from completing an anonymous manuscript review, and acknowledging and acting on this difference can have an impact on both the satisfaction and success of all concerned in the mentor relationship. The sample messages that start this chapter demonstrate in part the informal, personal nature of effective mentor/mentee relationships. In this chapter, then, we focus on this relationship as one of the most important in higher education.

This chapter addresses:

- The importance of mentoring
- Choosing who to advise/mentor
- Responsibilities of mentors
- Guidelines for mentoring
- The roles of technology in mentoring
- Listing mentoring on a CV or résumé

The Importance of Mentoring

Generally, the literature describes the *advising* relationship as a fairly prescriptive one, in which ideas such as which classes to take are discussed and the advisor has the final say. On the other hand, *mentoring* is seen as more supportive and developmental for students. In this view, advising can be seen as one aspect of the larger mentoring relationship. Some relationships with students stay at the advising stage, while others take on more of a mentoring aspect, which involves not only advising but a variety of additional facets discussed in what follows. The literature suggests that even a simple advising relationship can have an impact on student retention and satisfaction. For example, Pargett (2011) found in her study that students who have created a relationship with their assigned faculty advisor reported having

> more satisfaction with their college experience and positively develop as a student. In addition, students who perceived their advisor was using a developmental style of advising indicated that they were more satisfied with their college experience. The more a student and his or her advisor discussed personal and school-related issues, career options, college policies, academic deadlines, and study skills and tips, the more likely it was that the student positively developed and had a higher level of satisfaction with college.

> (p. ii)

In addition, Campbell and Nutt (2008) note that advising is "at the very core of successful student success initiatives, for it reflects an institution's commitment to the education of its students" (n.p.). They also suggest that, if the institution considers positive student learning outcomes as one goal of advising, then the advising/mentoring process can support both student and institutional success.

Benefits of Mentoring

Why mentor? In many institutions, advising/mentoring is seen as central service to the program and/or institution. Mentoring might be rewarded with course release time or other support, and effective mentoring might serve as outstanding informal advertising for the program or institution. Perhaps most important, the benefits for both mentor and mentee are many. For example, the extensive advising guide from the Rackham Graduate School at the University of Michigan (Rackham Graduate School, 2014) notes that students benefit from mentoring in that:

- It supports their advancement in research activity, conference presentations, publication, pedagogical skill, and grant-writing.
- Students are less likely to feel ambushed by potential bumps in the road, having been alerted to them, and provided resources for dealing with stressful or difficult periods in their graduate careers.
- The experiences and networks their mentors help them to accrue might improve the students' prospects of securing professional placement.
- The knowledge that someone is committed to their progress, someone who can give them solid advice and be their advocate, can help to lower stress and build confidence.
- Constructive interaction with a mentor and participation in collective activities he or she arranges promote engagement in the field. (p. 7)

Additional benefits for mentors include that

- Your students will keep you abreast of new knowledge and techniques and apprise you of promising avenues for research.
- A faculty member's reputation rests in part on the work of his or her former students; sending successful new scholars into the field increases your professional stature.

- Your networks are enriched. Helping students make the professional and personal connections they need to succeed will greatly extend your own circle of colleagues.
- Good students will be attracted to you. Word gets around about who the best mentors are, so they are usually the most likely to recruit—and retain—outstanding students.
- It's personally satisfying. Seeing your students succeed can be as rewarding as a major publication or significant grant.

(Rackham Graduate School, 2014, 7)

In other words, a developmental mentoring relationship can support the professional lives and careers of both parties, resulting not only in success in school and work but in e-mails like this one from a graduate student to her advisor:

I am writing this e-mail to express my gratitude for always being there to help me and other international students. Although you have a busy schedule, you have never ever hesitated to assist us. Amazed, inspired and grateful. That's how your generosity makes me feel. You are such a great professor. I have learned a lot from you. Thanks!

Choosing Who to Mentor

The first step in advising or mentoring is to decide who you want/need to mentor. Some organizations assign student advisees to faculty, while others allow faculty to choose. An appropriate mentee/mentor fit is important because it can determine the outcomes of the relationship. Because this relationship can last years and impact its members in so many ways, it is crucial to make sure it will work effectively.

At the undergraduate level, advising has traditionally consisted of helping students work out their schedules and checking that they have taken the correct classes; sometimes it also deals with helping mediate grade disputes and other conflicts.

Many universities have moved to centralized advising in which all undergraduate students are advised by professional advisors. The literature on advising best practices suggests clearly that undergraduates are in need of developmental advising (see, for example, a seminal article by Tinto, 1999), and some universities are moving in that direction. However, because undergraduate advisors generally are assigned students rather than choosing them, this section about choosing mentees deals mainly with graduate students.

Typically, when mentoring graduate students, faculty should choose students within their program whose interests are in the same general area as the faculty member's and/or whose research the faculty member feels s/he can make a contribution toward. It is also important for faculty to consider personalities when choosing students to mentor—if the student is not someone who can take the kind and format of advice the faculty member has to offer, that student might be better off being advised by someone else. There can still be conflicts, of course, and there are many good resources for helping solve them (see, for example Gordon, Habley, & Grites, 2011); however, it might be better to forestall time-wasting and perhaps unsolvable conflicts by choosing mentees carefully.

Another consideration is how much time a student might need for advising—international students, students with little background in the area or topic, or students who are new to research might need more time with their mentor than, say, a native-speaking student who has completed a master's thesis in the area (although there are certainly exceptions to this rule). How much time each student requires can also determine how many students one faculty member can effectively mentor.

In deciding with whom to work, mentors can ask students for résumés, previous publications or papers, and references from other academics and/or conduct a personal interview; if the choice is not the mentor's, it might still be useful to have this kind of information at hand. Additional information from students to help make decisions on whom to mentor can be garnered from the types of surveys that can be found on the website of the National Academic Advising Association (NACADA; http://nacada.ksu.edu).

Responsibilities of Mentors

Institutions and researchers have written a lot about the advising relationship, particularly at the undergraduate level. Although their ideas about what mentors need to do vary some, in general they are consistent in what they perceive the responsibilities of mentors to be. In some institutions these are mandated and measured; in others they are left to the mentor to decide.

Mentor responsibilities depend on the student level, program, and needs. One important aspect of mentoring is to understand that different students might experience college differently. Students might face a variety of challenges both related and unrelated directly to academics, particularly those from diverse sexual orientations, of different races and ethnicities, from varied first languages and cultures, and with backgrounds in poverty or experience with other social issues (these issues and some ways to address them are discussed more in depth in Gordon, Habley, & Grites, 2011 and other resources).

Overall, according to Gordon, Habley, and Grites (2011), effective mentors form caring relationships and promote student growth. Campbell and Nutt (2008) add that mentors are responsible for "setting high expectations, providing support, offering feedback, and facilitating involvement in learning through frequent student contact" (n.p.). More specific responsibilities might include monitoring student progress, choosing courses that fit student and programmatic goals, challenging mentees to do good work, making sure they know when paperwork is due, helping them choose a topic and research ideas that are appropriate in level of challenge and interest, providing practice in interviewing and other job techniques and requirements, and helping them figure out where to publish. The literature is clear that mentoring does not mean that the mentor spoon-feeds or directs the student—rather, it means participating in two-way dialogues to come to a mutually acceptable decision about whatever the focus is.

The University of Pittsburgh's University Council on Graduate Study adds that mentors should, as relevant:

- Assist students to develop grant writing skills, where appropriate.
- Educate students about research integrity and make them aware of the University's policies.
- Help students to develop artistic, analytical, interpretive, writing, verbal, quantitative and laboratory skills, where appropriate, in accordance with the expectations of the discipline.
- Encourage students to participate in professional meetings or perform or display their work in public settings.
- Help students gain an appreciation of teaching, assist students in improving their teaching skills, and provide them with guidance in how to prepare an appropriate teaching portfolio.
- Supply students with information about the variety of employment opportunities available to graduates of the program and encourage them to plan toward an employment goal as early in their course of graduate study as possible. (n.p.)

Again, mentoring might but does not necessarily need to include all the responsibilities listed above. Depending on the requirements and expectations of the institution and the people involved, mentoring relationships can appear quite different even within the same program.

Mentee Responsibilities

It is important to mention that the mentor/mentee relationship is not based solely on the mentor; students have responsibilities, too, that must be encouraged and supported. According to the University Council on Graduate Study at the University of Pittsburgh (www.pitt.edu/~graduate/advising.html) and others, these include that students should

- work on fulfilling their goals with necessary effort and an eye toward excellence;
- understand paperwork, timelines, and administrative requirements that are not the mentor's responsibility;
- pay attention to the mentor's workload and time constraints;
- come to sessions not only with questions but with potential answers and resources;
- ensure that the mentor is kept abreast of developments;
- be on time and ready for meetings and postpone or cancel with sufficient notice.

desJardins' (1994) advice on *How to Be a Good Graduate Student* still holds true and is useful reading for both students and mentors.

Guidelines for Mentoring

Gordon, Habley, and Grites (2011) suggest that mentors must start the mentoring relationship by getting off on the right foot. This includes greeting the student with a welcoming tone and using small talk to establish the developmental and personal nature of meetings. Once the tone is set, given the responsibilities noted previously, Stanford University (n.d.) notes that effective mentoring must be based on clear expectations and open communication. Most important, according to Gordon, Habley, and Grites (2011), is that both parties are willing to listen.

To help the mentoring relationship function smoothly and effectively, the literature suggests that mentors consider the following guidelines:

1. Let students set the agenda. Allowing students to choose the topics based on their needs and guiding rather than directing helps student growth. It also makes the relationship more equitable from the student standpoint and can keep meetings focused on important concerns. In the same vein, if the student asks for a meeting, it is useful to have an idea what the meeting will be about in order to prepare resources and whatever else might be needed. Sending a short e-mail message asking the student for an agenda ahead of time (or even just the meeting topic) can save time for both parties.

2. Set limits from the outset. Agree with the student specifically on questions such as how many times you are willing to read a paper, how much lead time you need to read, how much surface editing you are willing to do, what the student's responsibilities are, what yours are, and so on.

3. Help students find additional mentors. As students learn and experience, they might have questions that could better be answered by your colleagues or other experts whom you know. If you are the content expert for a student, the student might also need a mentor in research methods or some other area for which you know someone who could help.

4. Keep a folder on each student (electronic or paper) so that you know exactly what you told the student. If the institution or program does not already have such documents, use a worksheet or form to note students' short- and long-term goals, research questions in progress, concerns, and other things discussed.

5. Follow up each meeting with an e-mail, copied to your computer or printed for the student's folder, to highlight exactly what was said and agreed on. Ask the student to

acknowledge this message and to keep you current with the student's progress. This not only helps you remember where in the process you are with each student, but it can also help avoid conflicts because there is documentation.

6. Provide information and resources about what students can do and where they can go if they disagree or have conflicts. Let students know the "chain of command" in the program and institution and what authority you have (or do not have) to help solve certain kinds of conflicts. For example, students are generally asked to address the instructor for grade conflicts, but the mentor can be asked to participate in the discussion if the other parties agree. For sexual harassment and other conflicts students might have, the institution might have specific regulations that must be followed that might or might not involve the mentor.

There are no specific guidelines in the literature about how often mentors and mentees should meet, and this will depend on the needs of the student and the interest and available time of the mentor. However, mentors should meet with students enough to understand how they are progressing, and that means probably at least once per semester or quarter.

Another guideline found in the literature that is gaining more attention is using group advising. By meeting with more than one student in at least one meeting per semester, mentors can help students at the same or different levels form a cohort. This benefits both mentors and mentees in saving time on adminis-trivia and assuring that students all get the same information, and it allows time in one-on-one meetings to form developmental relationships between mentor and mentee. Supporting a mentee cohort also provides mentees with others to ask for help and information and with whom to discuss issues that might not affect mentors, such as course tasks and campus life.

Some of the advising literature cautions mentors that there can be a fine line between mentor and friend, but we believe that each relationship requires different levels and types of support and that being a "friend" happens naturally and usefully in many long-term mentoring relationships. Most institutions have guidelines for what is acceptable (and what is not) in a faculty/student relationship, but within these guidelines there is often much leeway for mentors to develop the relationship in both appropriate and long-lasting ways if they desire to. In other words, including an element of friendship in a mentoring relationship should not necessarily be considered cautionary.

Assessing the Relationship

Szymanska (2011) provides a variety of tools for measuring advising outcomes and notes that these should measure

1. Nature of the advising relationship,
2. Frequency of different types of activities that take place during advising sessions,
3. Students' satisfaction with academic advising,
4. Students' outcomes (increases in knowledge of academic environment, understanding of career goals, etc.),
5. Advisors' satisfaction. (p. 2)

While some institutions or programs will already have such measures in place, others will leave it up to the mentor and/or mentee to determine how the relationship is working out. By keeping notes on mentoring sessions and performing regular assessments on student progress, mentors can improve their relationships with students and thereby support achievement more effectively.

The Roles of Technology in Mentoring

Technology can play many roles in supporting the effectiveness and efficiency of a mentoring relationship. Its main role is not to replace face-to-face meetings but to supplement and complement those mentoring sessions. Some of the ways technology can support mentoring were mentioned earlier, such as asking students for a meeting agenda and following up with students after a mentoring session. However, there are many more options for using technology in mentoring.

First, e-mail is one efficient way for students to schedule meetings without actually having to stop by the office. Mentors could also use scheduling software such as Outlook (Microsoft) or Google Calendar for students to make appointments; the mentor could indicate available hours and have the students fill in their names and agendas from any digital device.

Other basic uses of technology in mentoring include using whatever software the institution uses in order to call up the latest versions of the student's transcripts and other documents that the institution has on line such as application letters, thesis paperwork, and other notifications. These can be used to remind the mentor of the student's status and to refer to during meetings to help make decisions. Another way to prepare for mentoring sessions is to "bookmark" Web pages that might be needed for reference so they can be accessed quickly.

Because one part of mentoring is making sure students can find the resources/outlets they need both within and external to the institution, the mentor (or even the mentees) might start a wiki page or other accessible forum where students can check a frequently-asked-question (FAQ) file; like face-to-face group advising, this can save time by having the same information available to all students.

In addition, mentors can use e-mail, texting, or SMS/chat for regular check-in messages with mentees. A monthly "Hi. What's up?" message can help keep students on track and mentors aware of any current issues. Another use of technology for mentors who review students' papers is to do so in Google Docs. Because the mentor and student can both see and edit the document once it is "shared," both can see the progress, and the mentor can provide instant feedback if the student is online at the same time. Because it does not require sending a document back and forth over e-mail (or commenting on paper copies that can be misplaced or forgotten), the Google document is always available online, and older versions can be referred to easily.

Finally, for group advising and online meetings, LinkedIn (www.linkedin.com/nhome/) and other social networks are popular forums and might also be used by students in their professional lives. Alternately, students can create and help each other through a Facebook page that the mentor can follow as needed. There are surely other ways to use technology to facilitate the developmental mentoring relationship, and these will develop as both the technology and the relationship do.

Listing Advising/Mentoring on a CV or Résumé

On an academic resume or vita, many faculty list their advisees in the service section under the subtitle "Advising," "Mentor Experience," or some similar category. Information that can be included is the first initial and last name of the advisee, the degree sought, the years advised, whether program and/or thesis advisor, and, if completed, date and title of thesis or dissertation. For example, an entry might be formatted like that in Figure 7.1.

Neither the American Psychological Association (APA) guide nor the Modern Language Association (MLA) standards

Figure 7.1 Entries for advising on an academic vita.

Master's Students

> **Program Director**
> Student name, program, completion date
> **Thesis Director**
> Student name, title of thesis, completion date
> **Committee Member**
> Student name, program and/or thesis committee, dates

Doctoral Students

> **Program Director**
> Student name, program, completion date
> **Dissertation Director**
> Student name, title of dissertation, completion date
> **Committee Member**
> Student name, program and/or dissertation committee, dates

say much about this topic, so for more examples, ask an experienced colleague or search "faculty résumé" in a web browser and choose from among the variety of formats.

Conclusion

Mentoring is an integral part of professional service, and it can play an important role in student and institutional success. Because every mentoring relationship is different, the guidelines and information in this chapter should be considered descriptive rather than prescriptive. However, the research shows clearly that effective mentoring can have an impact on student outcomes, particularly for traditionally underrepresented or challenged groups in higher education, and that a developmental approach is a sound basis for an effective mentoring relationship.

Recommended Resources

A great starting point for resources is the National Academic Advising Association (NACADA), an organization with members from around the globe. Resources available on their website include the following:

- *NACADA Clearinghouse of Academic Advising Resources*, available on the web at www.nacada.ksu.edu/Resources/Clearinghouse.aspx.

  The site includes articles and links that span the field of advising and cross disciplinary boundaries.

- *NACADA Journal.* Find information at www.nacada.ksu.edu/Resources/Journal.aspx.

  The journal features articles on advising research, theory, and practice.

- *Academic Advising Today: Voices of the Global Community.* Available at www.nacada.ksu.edu/Resources/Academic-Advising-Today.aspx.

  This is the quarterly publication of NACADA.

Guided Practice

1. Interview colleagues or professors about issues they have had with advising or mentoring and what information and advice they might give you about working with students from diverse backgrounds.
2. From your interviews, write up short scenarios to share with peers at a meeting or workshop regarding advising.

3. With colleagues, respond to the scenarios by answering questions like these (from Koring, 2003):
   - What aspects of the case are within the advisor's locus of control? What aspects are not?
   - What specific problems or issues are raised by this scenario?
   - What additional information might you need to handle the scenario? How would you get it?
   - What problems or issues would you refer? How?
   - What problems or issues could/should you address yourself? How?

References

Campbell, S., & Nutt, C. (2008). Academic advising in the new global century: Supporting student engagement and learning outcomes achievement. *Peer Review, 10*(1), n.p.

desJardins, M. (1994). *How to be a good graduate student.* Retrieved 22 August 2015 from www.cs.indiana.edu/how.2b/how.2b.html

Gordon, V., Habley, W., & Grites, T. (Eds.). (2011). *Academic advising: A comprehensive handbook* (2nd ed.). San Francisco: Wiley/Jossey-Bass.

Koring, H. (2003, December). The justification for case studies in advisor training and development. *Academic Advising Today, 26*(4), n.p.

Pargett, K. (2011). *The effects of faculty advising on college student development in higher education* (Unpublished master's thesis). University of Nebraska. Retrieved 22 August 2015 from http://digitalcommons.unl.edu/cgi/view content.cgi?article=1083&context=cehsedaddiss

Rackham Graduate School. (2014). *How to mentor graduate students: A guide for faculty.* Ann Arbor: Regents of the University of Michigan.

Stanford University Office of the Vice Provost for Graduate Education. (n.d.). *Advising and Mentoring.* Retrieved 22 August 2015 from https://vpge. stanford.edu/academic-guidance/advising-mentoring

Szymanska, I. (2011). *Best practices for evaluating academic advising.* Retrieved 22 August 2015 from http://advising.uncc.edu/sites/advising.uncc.edu/ files/media/Best-Practices-Evaluating-Academic-Advising.pdf

Tinto, V. (1999, Fall). Taking retention seriously: Rethinking the first year of college. *NACADA Journal, 19*(2), 5–9.

University Council on Graduate Study, Office of the Provost, University of Pittsburgh. (n.d.). *Elements of good academic advising.* Retrieved 22 August 2015 from www.pitt.edu/~graduate/advising.html

8

PROVIDING INTERNAL AND EXTERNAL PROFESSIONAL DEVELOPMENT

Excerpt from a funded professional development grant proposal:

In the project outlined in this proposal, we intend to

1) extend beyond the existing professional development in reading for classroom teachers of English language learners (ELLs) that was developed through a [previous] grant. We plan to help teachers involve parents in the reading achievement of their children;
2) provide a model for language minority learner/parent involvement in schools, and;
3) develop responsible, effective, technologically-enhanced partnerships between teachers and parents of ELLs.

Overview

In previous chapters we discussed several types of service that can also be part of providing professional development

(PD) for peers and others. For example, reviewing and editing manuscripts can be a developmental experience for colleagues (Chapter 3), as can making presentations in a variety of forums (Chapter 2). In fact, many of the guidelines for mentoring (Chapter 7) also apply to the professional development of colleagues and peers, and PD can be supported by grants for service projects (Chapter 9), as demonstrated by the opening excerpt. However, there are additional considerations that come into play when providing professional development as a service for colleagues and K–12 educators.

This chapter addresses:

- Professional development as service
- Types of professional development
- Guidelines for PD
- The roles of technology in PD
- Listing PD on a CV or résumé

Professional Development as Service

The term *professional development* indicates opportunities to acquire new knowledge and/or skills related to one's profession. Typically PD is provided by an "expert" in the area of interest. PD can occur any time during or after a person has begun working on the initial requirements for the profession; for example, teachers or administrators in their first year of teaching might participate in PD, as might full professors who have been in academia for many years but want to learn something new or brush up on skills they already have.

Those who *provide* professional development might do so as a result of receiving a grant, in response to a request from an administrator or program coordinator, because a need is seen, because it is part of the institution's program, and for other reasons. Those who *participate* in PD might do so as a requirement to keep or obtain certification, from their own interest, or for any number of other reasons. As with other activities categorized as service, some institutions will give credit toward yearly work goals for providing or participating in professional development experiences, while others will not; this might depend on whether data is collected or other research is a part of the plan. We propose that, as educators, providing PD is an essential part of the work we do and that all or most of PD should be considered important service to the institution and field. As always, before embarking on this kind of work, PD providers and participants need to be sure the benefits to all stakeholders outweigh the disadvantages.

Types of Professional Development

Professional development can take many forms. For example, PD can be internal or external. Internal PD is provided for colleagues, teacher education students, and other employees of an institution, while external PD is for communities outside the institution such as school staff and administrators, the public, and even legislators. In addition, PD can be formal or informal. Formal PD might be assignment to a required faculty mentoring committee or providing a structured in-service workshop for teachers. Informal PD includes more fluid types of forums and interactions such as online professional communities of practice, accessing websites with information, holding individual conversations with experts, and so on. Formal PD experiences can typically be listed on a résumé as service more easily than informal PD, but those who do any kind of PD as service should check on the guidelines of their institution and field.

Topics for PD depend on the audience and context. For example, lawmakers might want to better understand the workings of a college of education before they implement new regulations or requirements, while school administrators might want help understanding how to best implement state requirements already in place. Teachers might ask for assistance working with an increasingly diverse school demographic, whereas higher education peers might want to better understand the use of technology for student learning. Formats for PD differ as widely as the topics, from a one-hour brown-bag lunch to a weekend workshop to guidance offered over time. Each of these forums requires different roles and strategies, but overall they should adhere to the guidelines in this (and other) chapters.

Benefits of Providing PD

Providing professional development, especially in an internal collegial mentoring relationship, is important to education institutions in many ways. For example, having this kind of support promotes faculty retention, helps faculty understand the institutional context and procedures, and provides awareness of what the institution and colleagues expect (which are sometimes not the same). PD for external school participants can help them create professional networks and provide faculty with insight into "real" classrooms, understand other needs to be met, and gain support for implementing innovation. PD presented for members of the public can help them understand both higher education and K–12 schools, and the same goes for lawmakers and other educational stakeholders. All this PD can ultimately affect student achievement by helping to improve educational environments and supporting collaboration among stakeholders, because, as Mizell (2010) notes,

> Teachers and administrators who routinely develop their own knowledge and skills model for students that learning is important and useful. Their ongoing development creates a culture of learning throughout the school and supports educators' efforts to engage students in learning.

> (p. 18)

These are certainly goals worth pursuing for any education faculty member.

Guidelines for PD

This section divides the guidelines for PD into two parts: (1) faculty mentoring and (2) professional development for external stakeholders such as teachers and administrators. Many of the principles apply to providing PD for these and other groups.

For Internal Colleagues/Peers

To the general benefits of providing PD mentioned, Pierce (2015) adds that mentoring other faculty can provide more experienced faculty with an "infusion of excitement" (n.p.). Mentoring peers can be similar to but is not the same as mentoring students. Not only is the power relationship different, but the differences in age and knowledge between faculty and students can make a difference in their needs and wants. While Pierce (2015) differentiates between "primary" mentoring, which she defines as a hierarchical expert/apprentice approach between senior and junior faculty, and "peer" mentoring, which is characterized as a narrower relationship between colleagues at the same level, it might be more effective for all faculty to consider mentoring as a complementary benefit and work to provide a comprehensive, two-way approach as far as possible.

Penner (2001) notes that there are many elements of mentoring peers that participants in the mentoring relationship should be aware of. These elements are listed in Figure 8.1. Mentor pairs or groups can use this list to help them understand and plan for their relationship.

Caddick (2009) offers a very complete and useful mentoring workbook that is filled with important information for faculty mentors. Along with other useful information and handouts,

Figure 8.1   Elements of mentoring from Penner (2001, p. 46).

Elements of Mentoring

The elements of a mentoring relationship have numerous permutations.

- **Initiation.** Such a relationship may be initiated by a mentor, the mentee, or a third party such as Academic Dean.
- **Time frame.** The relationship may be time limited, lifelong or open-ended.
- **Formality.** The relationship may be quite informal or may involve an articulated, jointly forged formal agreement.
- **Intensity.** Participants may connect only occasionally or meet regularly according to a prescribed schedule.
- **Reciprocity.** The relationship may be viewed as substantially in place to benefit the mentee or ... be seen as mutually beneficial and power-free.
- **Agenda.** The agenda for the relationship may be quite focused on professional matters or more holistically include other aspects of life. Generally, the mentee's agenda is considered primary, but in cases of a more reciprocal relationship, there will be more balance in agenda focus.
- **Medium.** Most often, mentoring relationships are face-to-face. However, there is an emergence of mediated connection via telephone and e-mail.

it includes a mentoring readiness assessment, sample mentoring contract, action plan, and tips and strategies for mentors and mentees. Use of at least some of these ideas can help a mentoring relationship get off on the right foot and continue to flourish. Caddick reminds mentors that adults learn and interact in different ways from younger people and that the mentoring relationship should be based on these principles. They include:

- Adults learn best when they are involved in diagnosing, planning, implementing, and evaluating their own learning.
- The role of the facilitator is to create and maintain a supportive climate that promotes the conditions necessary for learning to take place.
- Adults have a need to be self-directing.
- Readiness for learning increases when there is a specific need to know.
- Life's reservoir of experience is a primary learning resource; the life experiences of others add enrichment to the learning process.
- Adult learners have an inherent need for immediacy of application.
- Adults respond best to learning when they are internally motivated to learn.

(Caddick, 2009, p. 9)

In order to act according to these principles, mentors must take the time to get to know their faculty mentees. Working out a mentoring contract not only allows mentees control over their work but can also help keep the relationship moving in a positive way. In addition to applicable guidelines for mentoring from Chapter 7, another guideline that can help to insure a supportive relationship includes discussing how the interaction will go during mentoring sessions, whether formal or informal. For example, a mentor who typically advises by giving a series of short speeches might have an issue with a mentee who learns by interrupting and clarifying. In addition, acknowledging both mentor and mentee expertise can facilitate a relationship less burdened by power or other issues. Finally, because mentors commonly share foundational knowledge and/or interest in a specific field, working to present or publish together can be mutually beneficial and strengthen the relationship. Mentoring does not have to take a lot of time if the needs of the mentee are not great. Many profitable mentoring relationships take place on an informal "drop-in" basis, and this can include senior faculty in one area assisting those in another. For example, a professor might e-mail another that they have a quick question, and the response might be to drop in any time or to come during office hours or to meet for coffee. Similarly, if a junior faculty member has a question for a senior faculty member that can be answered simply and quickly, they might be able to have their question answered by walking over to the mentor's office for a brief chat. Whether a question or issue needs to be addressed with more time and effort varies, and that decision should be up to both members in the relationship.

As when mentoring students, not all faculty mentoring relationships will work out. Personality differences, time issues, a lack of willingness, ideological disagreements, and other issues might prove to be barriers to the relationship. The mentor agreeing gracefully to sever the relationship and help the mentee find a more appropriate mentor might lead to greater mentee growth.

For External Stakeholders

According to the LearningForward Association (http://learning forward.org, n.d.) and much of the research literature on professional development, "For most educators working in schools, professional learning is the singular most accessible means they have to develop the new knowledge, skills, and practices necessary to better meet students' learning needs" (n.p.). There is certainly a plethora of literature that addresses effective teacher professional development, including theoretical papers and research studies, state and district guidelines and requirements, and principles and standards proposed by professional education organizations. Unfortunately, not all the literature agrees on what best practices are; that makes sense, because different people and contexts require different information and support. However, the literature is very clear that one-time, one-size-fits-all PD is not usually effective in supporting change. Consistent follow-up and feedback such as that which can be supplied by in-school coaches appears to be more beneficial, although not always feasible. Overall though, according to Mizell (2010),

Effective professional development enables educators to develop the knowledge and skills they need to address students' learning challenges. To be effective, professional development requires thoughtful planning followed by careful implementation with feedback to ensure it responds to educators' learning needs. Educators who participate in professional development then must put their new knowledge and skills to work. Professional development is not effective unless it causes teachers to improve their instruction or causes administrators to become better school leaders.

(p. 10)

The LearningForward Association (http://learningforward.org/ standards-for-professional-learning#.Vbfcf3nbJwK) provides the following general standards for professional learning for teachers, administrators, and PD providers to consider:

Communities

Professional learning that increases educator effectiveness and results for all students occurs within learning communities committed to continuous improvement, collective responsibility, and goal alignment.

Leadership

Professional learning that increases educator effectiveness and results for all students requires skillful leaders who develop capacity, advocate, and create support systems for professional learning.

Resources

Professional learning that increases educator effectiveness and results for all students requires prioritizing, monitoring, and coordinating resources for educator learning.

Data

Professional learning that increases educator effectiveness and results for all students uses a variety of sources and types of student, educator, and system data to plan, assess, and evaluate professional learning.

Learning Designs

Professional learning that increases educator effectiveness and results for all students integrates theories, research, and models of human learning to achieve its intended outcomes.

Implementation

Professional learning that increases educator effectiveness and results for all students applies research on change and sustains support for implementation of professional learning for long-term change.

Outcomes

Professional learning that increases educator effectiveness and results for all students aligns its outcomes with educator performance and student curriculum standards.

(n.p.)

One way to meet these standards for providing effective PD is to consider how the PD plan meets the research-based guidelines for situated learning that have been shown to be effective in a variety of contexts (see, for example, Egbert & Salsbury, 2009). These guidelines include that the PD provides

- authentic contexts that reflect the way the knowledge will be used in real life;
- authentic activities;
- access to expert performances and the modeling of processes;
- multiple roles and perspectives;
- promotion of reflection and articulation;
- authentic assessment of learning within the tasks.

(Egbert & Salsbury, 2009, p. 377)

An example of PD that is framed around these concepts is provided in Appendix 8-A; this framework can be used during planning, implementation, or assessment of a PD project.

To help insure PD that meets these guidelines, PD providers can involve their audience in every aspect of the PD process. With participants, they can

- clarify specific improvements in performance that are needed,
- detail the learning outcomes expected and how these might occur,
- determine steps that might lead to different levels of improvement,
- ask educators and others what the real challenges they face are and try to observe them firsthand,
- survey teachers to understand their motivations, interests, knowledge, and current skills,
- treat teachers and other attendees as the experts they are,
- provide time and space for attendees to discuss among themselves,
- assess each step of the PD process, from organization to outcomes.

Supporting participants to be active in their own PD can provide a firm foundation for addressing their differing needs, abilities, and wants.

Additional Ideas About PD

There are a number of issues with providing PD that providers should be aware of. For example, while the federal government might require a certain procedure for grants supporting PD, teachers might desire something completely different, and the research might suggest another thing entirely. Integrating the needs and requirements of all stakeholders requires time and care.

Another issue is how to help graduate students, as future faculty members, learn to provide effective professional development for teachers and other education stakeholders. This can happen in many ways during graduate coursework, but the situated learning model outlined earlier suggests that students should have the opportunity to plan and carry out PD while they are learning about it. The assignment worksheet in Appendix 8-A2 can serve as a starting point for faculty to develop various tasks that challenge students to research and provide PD to their peers.

An additional issue is whether K–12 students should be involved in professional development for educators and other education stakeholders. At times, this might not seem the best thing to do, for example, because teachers do not want to admit their lack of knowledge or administrators do not feel that students need to be involved in the running of the school. However, since the hoped-for outcomes for much external PD involve students, it seems logical that students would have a role in this PD by providing reactions and feedback, serving as part of demonstrations, or acting as part of planning teams. The decision about whether to include students should involve all relevant stakeholders.

The Roles of Technology in PD

Technology can play many roles in supporting the effectiveness and efficiency of PD. For example, mentors can keep in touch via social networks, and institutional websites can be accessed for information. Mentors might use technology to demonstrate a concept or as the topic of a session. For external PD, Johnson (2015) suggests using tools such as Google Forms, Padlet, and Nearpod to gain information from teachers and others to help shape the PD experience. Depending on the audience and context, PowerPoint, Prezi, or Powtoon might be used as both a presentation tool and a learning environment. Applications that provide interactivity among participants both during and after the initial PD include Skype, e-mail, instant messaging, and even Twitter. Further, websites can provide content for PD participants, and they can also be used to demonstrate concepts that are part of the PD focus. Overall, technology can help participants in PD communicate, demonstrate, present, evaluate, and much more.

Listing Professional Development on a CV or Résumé

Professional development can be listed on a CV in many ways, depending on what the service actually is and preferences in the institution and/or academic area. For mentoring, information that can be included is the first initial and last name of the advisee, rank, the years advised, and whether assigned or chosen. If the PD is external based on a grant, it might be listed both under grants and under the service category, or it might be listed under only one. School-based PD could also be listed under presentations; because there is no hard-and-fast rule, providers should consider where the information would be most relevant in the CV or résumé. For example, PD entries might be formatted like those in Figure 8.2.

See other chapters in this text for ways to list presentations, editing/reviewing, mentoring, and other types of service included in or a result of professional development.

Figure 8.2 Sample vita entries for PD providers.

Mentoring Committees

2015–2016 *Committee member,* Dr. M. Smith, Assistant Professor of School Counseling.

2012–2014 *Chair,* Dr. A. Barrio, Associate Professor of Higher Education Administration.

In-Service or Other Professional Development

2016 *Scaffolded reading experiences.* In-service for Jones Middle School, Central City, in partial fulfillment of the Smith Education Grant, February 11.

2015 *ESL in the content area classroom: Every Student Learns.* In-service for Franklin Junior High, Central City, with C. Thomas & H. Hayes, March 2.

Conclusion

Providing professional development has many benefits and some potential pitfalls, but done well, it can help colleagues, teachers, administrators, and community members engage in schools and learning from a knowledgeable, collaborative perspective.

Recommended Resources

- *Edutopia.* Available at www.edutopia.org/blogs/tag/profession al-development

  Videos, articles, blog posts and other information for teacher professional development.

- Felten, P., Bauman, H., Kheriaty, A., Taylor, E., Palmer, P. (2013). *Transformative conversations: A guide to mentoring communities among colleagues in higher education.* San Francisco, CA: Jossey-Bass.

- YouTube video: *Transformative conversations: A guide to mentoring communities among colleagues in higher education* at www.youtube.com/watch?v=hoabY-erUsI
  This video explores issues from the Felten et al. text listed above.

Guided Practice

1. Choose a PD session that you have created or read about, and fill in the handout in Appendix 8-A1 about it. What's missing? What could be done better?
2. Use the PD workshop handout in Appendix 8-B to develop a plan for a workshop for peers.
3. Use the recommended resources above to add or change the elements in Appendix 8-A1. Discuss your changes with colleagues/peers.

References

Caddick, P. (2009). *Who is holding the rope for you? Building effective mentoring relationships: Mentoring workbook.* Retrieved 22 August 2015 from http://pcaddick.com/Mentoring%20workbook/Full%20mentoring%20workbook%20for%20PDF%20link.pdf

Egbert, J., & Salsbury, T. (2009). "Out of complacency and into action": An exploration of professional development experiences in school/home literacy engagement. *Teaching Education, 20*(4), 375–393. DOI: 10.1080/10476210902998474

Johnson, L. (2015, January 22). *Using pre-needs assessment for effective PD.* Retrieved 22 August 2015 from www.edutopia.org/blog/pre-needs-assessment-effective-pd-lisa-johnson

Mizell, H. (2010). *Why professional development matters.* Oxford, OH: Learning Forward. Retrieved 22 August 2015 from http://learningforward.org/docs/pdf/why_pd_matters_web.pdf?sfvrsn=0

Penner, R. (2001). Mentoring in higher education. *Direction, 30*(1), 45–52.

Pierce, G. (2015). *Mentoring: Functions, roles, and interactions.* National Education Association, (n.p). Retrieved 22 August 2015 from www.nea.org/home/34958.htm

Table of Situated Learning Elements From Egbert & Salsbury (2009)

Table 1 Project activities alignment with situated learning elements.

Situated learning element	Project activity
Provide authentic context that reflects the way the knowledge will be used in real life	The context was the teachers' own classrooms. They worked with colleagues within their schools and districts and with other teachers throughout the state who were facing the same issues. Each individual task was created based upon the school curriculum for the specific grade level and the state standards for literacy and content-learning.
Provide authentic activities	Activities for the teachers included reading and discussion, creating student tasks, assessing, and reflecting—all central to teachers' classroom lives
Provide access to expert performances and the modeling of processes	University faculty worked as facilitators and encouragers so that teachers/schools could find ways that suited their own contexts. Through two to three face-to-face

Situated learning element	Project activity
	meetings and consistent interaction within the electronic discussion forum, faculty provided constant advice and support of all kinds.
Provide multiple roles and perspectives	Teachers shared their thoughts and experiences via an electronic discussion system. Each district noted the individual complexities that they were dealing with and compared and contrasted those with teachers in the other districts.
Promote reflection and articulation	Collaborative groupings of teachers, a complex task, and opportunities to publicly present successes and failures promoted both reflection and articulation within the electronic discussion. Participant contact averaged 80 hours over the project year, including face-to-face visits, e-mail exchanges and phone calls, and electronic forum discussions. Teacher participants made 319 total entries in the discussion forum, and many more were made by faculty. This is an average of 19 postings per teacher-participant. In addition, teacher-participants made 564 viewings of postings, an average of 33 per teacher-participant. This clearly shows not only active involvement but constant interaction among participants.
Provide for authentic assessment of learning within the tasks	Teachers evaluated both their students' outcomes and their own pedagogical decisions. Faculty collected parent, teacher, and student surveys (see Appendix B for the teacher survey form), e-mails, and meeting notes, and the electronic forum data to use in evaluating the project. A follow-up survey was also administered to teachers during the semester following the end of the project.

Situated Learning Elements Handout

Situated Learning Element	Project Activity
Provide authentic context that reflects the way the knowledge will be used in real life	
Provide authentic activities	
Provide access to expert performances and the modeling of processes	
Provide multiple roles and perspectives	
Promote reflection and articulation	
Provide for authentic assessment of learning within the tasks	

*Graduate Student Professional Development
Workshop Outline*

Part 1

Instructions:

1. Based on the readings, fieldwork, and discussion in this course, reflect briefly on the attitudes and/or actions of teachers and other school personnel that could be more conducive to the language development and academic success of linguistic and cultural minorities.
2. Interview or survey other students in your appointed group about their attitudes and understandings of language development and academic success. In a word-processing file, write a short (one-paragraph) description or list of attitudes and actions of your participants that you believe to be the most significant challenges for their English language learners.

3. Brainstorm possible ways to help yourself and your participants become aware of and overcome these barriers. Write the ideas you brainstormed in a paragraph in the same file as your description of teacher attitudes.

Part 2

Instructions: Now that you are aware of the substantial impact teacher attitudes and actions can have on the linguistic and academic success of English language learners, design a plan for a one- to three-hour workshop to help other teachers (in your group) increase their awareness in one area. Design the workshop so that it is especially relevant for the participants in your group. Suggested (but not required) elements for your workshop include:

- A goal statement
- A focus activity for participants
- Presentations of relevant information
- Awareness-enhancing activities
- Strategy-enhancing activities
- Reflection and discussion questions
- Assessment of understanding

Part 3

Instructions: In a paragraph, summarize how the handouts, activities, presentations, and/or other tasks in your workshop will help meet your intended goals; refer to the literature. Then explain what the next step in your PD plan would be.

9

GRANT-MAKING AS SERVICE

From an award letter from an internal grant competition:

> Through the efforts of the Teaching Academy and the Office of Under-graduate Education, I am pleased to award you an e-Learning grant in the amount of $3583 for [your project]. The funds must be expended [within a year].

Overview

A funding award letter is one of the nicest professional letters to receive, because it implies that you have an idea worth supporting and allots the support to carry out that idea. Many institutions consider grants as scholarship rather than service, but for us and other institutions, how it is recognized depends on the focus and amount of the funding. There are many sources of information across the Internet for faculty and students who want to obtain funding; this chapter presents an overview of the process and resources to help get started. This chapter addresses:

- Grant-making as service
- Guidelines for grant-making
- Publishing from a grant
- Listing grants on a CV or résumé

Grant-Making as Service

There are many different kinds of funding educators can apply for, from million-dollar-plus, 3-year federal grants to $50 materials grants from nonprofit organizations. Universities often distinguish between grants in two ways—determining whether they are "large" or "small" (often using an arbitrary cutoff) and deciding based on the proposed grant activities whether they are "research" grants or more applied "project" grants. In many universities, research grants are counted as scholarship; some also include large project grants as scholarship, but it is more common that grants that focus on, say, teacher or materials development would be considered service. Grant-funded service projects can run the gamut from developing and implementing curriculum for educational institutions in other countries to creating new computer applications for student learning to providing horse-riding lessons for local children with physical challenges. Some funding organizations will support discipline-based course materials development, while others might provide technologies to make implementing pedagogical innovations easier. Some organizations provide cash, while others provide material or resource assistance. As with any type of service, it is important before getting started on a grant to understand the individual institution's guidelines and expectations for grant work and how the institution will "count" funding obtained.

Typically, in large doctoral-granting universities, faculty are encouraged to pursue research grants, but there are certainly valid reasons to go after project funding. For example, while some organizations, such as the National Science Foundation (NSF), the Institute for Education Sciences (IES), and the U.S. State Department generally fund only large research grants that are a fit with their guidelines and priorities, smaller funding from professional organizations and foundations might not have such focused requirements. In addition, after funding has been obtained from one organization, it might be easier to obtain funding from others because of the record of success. A project grant could help the participants uncover or better understand some phenomenon, and this understanding could be applied to obtaining a large research grant on the topic. Further, funding from local organizations might be easier to obtain than large research grants and require a far shorter application and review process. Moreover, local teachers, parents, and students might be more willing to participate in an applied project rather than serving as participants in a study. Finally, projects can be written up and published for a variety of refereed and other journals, particularly if they address innovation and have outcomes attached. In other words, there are many reasons to look for grants as service.

Just as there are benefits to obtaining project funding, there are also caveats. Some institutions might actively discourage faculty from looking for this kind of funding, and others might not reward sufficiently the actual time and energy put forth in both obtaining and implementing such projects. Sometimes local partners, often required as participants in the grant project, do not get their letters of support and other materials in on time, and sometimes they do not uphold their responsibilities as partners. In addition, from the time the proposal is sent to the actual funding period many things can change, and sometimes ideas have to be rethought or revised. Overall, however, obtaining grant funding to provide service to education can be not only fulfilling but of immediate use to the community where the project takes place.

Guidelines for Grant-Making

The guidelines that follow do not cover every aspect of grant-making. However, the steps outlined below provide a succinct overview to help grant seekers figure out the basic process. Some of the steps might be iterative, and they often occur simultaneously or in a different sequence, but the content is similar across most grant applications. We assume that the grant seeker will thoroughly review institutional guidelines and processes before applying for funding.

Before Writing

The most important work on a grant often takes place before the proposal is written. The first step is to figure out the project focus and whether the project is worth doing (and is possible to do). Reading the relevant literature, having conversations with potential partners, and having the project idea reviewed by knowledgeable faculty and administrators are effective ways to get started.

In conjunction with the first step, external partners should be tapped; these can include teachers, administrators, students, schools, community members, businesses, and others who have a vested interest in the project. Sometimes service grants in education require K–12 teachers to play the primary role; however, teachers often do not know where to apply for funding or even that funding is available for their great idea. Faculty can partner with teachers to provide information, resources, writing support, and grant administration and implementation. Partners should be vetted carefully to ensure not only that they provide input and understand their roles but also that they will continue the project until it ends, provide needed paperwork, and perform administrative duties as needed. Many funded projects fail because one or more of the partners does not fulfill its obligations.

The next step is to choose one or more funders. Universities might have internal grant competitions based on a request for proposals (RFP) like the one in Appendix 9-A. These are a useful place to vet your ideas and, because they are offered by your institution, there should be a lot of support for proposal writers. Foundations, businesses, state education agencies, and professional organizations might also fund service projects. Relatively new but equally viable sources for funding include public funding sites such as GoFundMe (www.gofundme.com/) and Kickstarter (www.kickstarter.com/; see Noonoo, 2015, for information). There are many ways to find funders, but the simplest is probably to do a Web search. Figure 9.1 shows websites that provide lists of funders and Figure 9.2 provides a screen shot of some of the grant funders listed on grantsalert.com (www.grantsalert.com). Figure 9.3 presents a list of some of the foundations and corporations that conduct grant programs. During this step of the grant-making process, it might be useful to contact the program officer for the grant funding under consideration; the officer might be able to tell you if your idea is fundable and can provide more details about the funding process. In addition, grant personnel exist at many institutions and might have inside information about the funding organization.

There are also many local and state organizations that fund within a certain jurisdiction (for example, for a list of funders by state, check the Grantsmanship Center, www.tgci.com/funding-sources).

Figure 9.1 Websites that provide lists of funders.

Source	Content	Other
Grantsalert.com	Corporation, foundation, state, and federal grant competitions for K–12 teachers	Site is free; grant-writing help is provided
Getedfunding.com	All levels, all funders	Some free samples; site registration required
U.S. Department of Education (www2.ed.gov/ programs/find/elig/ index.html)	Different level RFPs for specifically-focused projects	Only some are service projects
GrantWatch.com	Higher education and nonprofit organizations	Not all are focused on education
Edutopia.com www.edutopia. org/grants-and- resources#graph1	Grants for teachers	Also resources, contests, and classroom guides

Figure 9.2 Screenshot of grant competitions on grantsalert.com.

Latest Grants:

Green Thumb Challenge Grant
Deadline Sep 30, 15

Donald Samull Classroom Herb Garden Grant
Deadline Oct 01, 15

Invest in Youth Grantmaking Program
Deadline Jun 30, 15

Healthy Smiles, Healthy Children Grants
Deadline Oct 19, 15

Before deciding which funder(s) to write the proposal for, grant-seekers should read the RFP very carefully and see if it fits with the project intentions and whether the requirements of

Figure 9.3 Examples of corporate and foundation funders.

- Edutopia.org
- Paul G. Allen Family Foundation
- Bank of America
- Ford Foundation
- Bill and Melinda Gates Foundation
- W. M. Keck Foundation
- Google
- Kresge Foundation
- Paul Lauzier Foundation
- Henry Luce Foundation
- Microsoft
- M. J. Murdock Charitable Trust
- Procter & Gamble
- Starbucks
- Verizon Foundation

the RFP can be met. For example, some funders might request monthly reports, and faculty might not have time to provide these. Others require visits from program officers to the project site or a certain number of hours spent on specific parts of the project. If the RFP is not a good fit or requires changes in the original idea that the funding seeker is not prepared to make, alternate RFPs should be sought.

Writing the Proposal

How a proposal should be written and what it should contain depend on the requirements of the funder. For example, Appendix 9-B provides a funded proposal aimed at an internal institutional grant competition; as part of the proposal the institution required the application to state how the project meets the institution's strategic priorities. Appendix 9-C presents a letter of interest (LOI) for a foundation grant; this one-page project overview also served as the proposal. These two examples show some of the potential differences in proposal requirements among funders; however, there are also common elements among RFPs, noted in Figure 9.4.

When writing the proposal, the most important guideline is to follow the specifications of the funding organization exactly. This includes keeping to any page limits and font sizes set and including the information requested (no more and no less). Many organizations will ask that proposal writers use language that a layperson (someone not in the profession) could understand; one way to insure this is to have a layperson review the proposal for any language that is overly academic or contains field-specific jargon. Often, if the RFP instructions are not followed precisely, the proposal will not be considered.

Another important guideline is to include a sound theoretical framework for the project. Although not all RFPs explicitly state that this is necessary, the project summary and narrative should have a brief but solid grounding in both the relevant

Figure 9.4 Common request for proposals (RFP) elements.

Common Request for Proposals (RFP) Elements

- Proposal
- Project summary/narrative
- Assessment narrative
- Expected outcomes
- Budget and budget narrative
- Brief résumés
- Other potential support for the project
- Letters of support
- Additional materials as required by the call for proposals

literature and past successful projects so proposal readers can see that the project is based in a firm foundation.

When writing the budget, if required, again the most important consideration is what the funder wants. Asking for something that it does not fund (e.g., construction or capital purchases) might get the proposal disqualified. It is important to read the budget instructions carefully and perhaps consult with an institutional expert to make sure the budget and the budget narrative (an explanation of the expenditures) are clear and accurate according to the RFP requirements.

Project Implementation

Finally, in implementing the project, it is important that the project implementation follows the approved proposal; this means, for example, that the budget is spent as described in the proposal and that good records are kept in cases of inquiries. If changes need to be made, an inquiry to the funder will often result in agreement.

During and after the project, most project funders will expect some kind of report about how the money was spent and what the outcomes were. An example of a final report format for a state project grant can be found in Appendix 9-D.

Additional Guidelines

In addition to the guidelines listed, there are several others that can support successful grant-making. First, grant seekers must plan ahead. This is particularly true if letters of support, signatures, and other grant pieces must be obtained from a variety of participants; this part of the process can take longer than expected, and whoever needs to sign off might not be available at a convenient time. Second, proposals must be thoroughly spell-checked and proofread. A proposal with surface errors can make it look unprofessional and as if the writer does not pay attention to details—this can spell disaster for the proposal. Finally, if the proposal is not funded, the grant seeker can ask for comments about the proposal from the funding organization. Not all organizations will agree to do this, and it might take some time for organizations that do agree to respond, but these comments can be invaluable in seeking future funding.

Publishing From a Grant

There are many ways to publish from service projects. To begin with, describing the project in newspapers and newsletters can help spread information about the work on a ground level. In addition, practitioner-focused journals such as *TESOL Journal*, *The Science Teacher*, and *The Reading Teacher* accept manuscripts based on practice. Faculty can work with grant participants to write conceptual and how-to pieces, and assessment data can be used to provide data for more research- or outcomes-focused articles. Happily, because the proposal itself probably already contains the theoretical framework and project narrative, any article that comes from the project might already be half written.

Listing Grants on a CV or Résumé

As with mentoring, there is not one specific way to list grant funding on a résumé. A general expectation is that grants that were not funded are not included (however, they might be included in other paperwork, such as the annual review from the department, other internal evaluations, or a very inclusive curriculum vita). For grants that are funded, the most recent are listed first, just like employment and publications. Basic information usually included in listing a grant on a résumé is: year awarded, principal investigator(s) (PIs) or project team members, title of the project

Figure 9.5 Sample entry for funded grants on a résumé.

2015 Egbert, J., Barrio, B., Lamb, R., & Skavdahl, S. *Helping teachers create resource-rich, student-centered flipped learning: Focus on video production.* Stubblefield Foundation, $3000, funded 2014–2015.

2013 Egbert, J. *Supporting pre-service teacher understandings and experiences: Active, sustainable learning in the flipped classroom.* Samuel H. and Patricia W. Smith Teaching and Learning Endowment 2013. $6,000 funded 4/1/13–4/1/14.

(if there is one), funder, years covered by the grant, and amount funded. The order of these items can move around, but entries might look something like those in Figure 9.5.

The Purdue OWL (https://owl.english.purdue.edu/owl/resource/641/01/) and other resources have additional tips on where and how to include grant funding on a professional vita.

Conclusion

Although a lot of important research is conducted with large grants from organizations such as the NSF and IES, equally important teaching, learning, and innovating practice can be achieved through service projects with any amount of funding. Whether from an internal competition, a professional organization, or a large corporate foundation, service project funding can make a difference in the lives of teachers, students, and faculty, and that makes it worth seeking.

Recommended Resources

- Browning, B. (2007). *Perfect phrases for writing grant proposals.* Columbus, OH: McGraw-Hill.

This book shows proposal writers how to structure their proposal, providing example paragraphs for each aspect of a proposal. Useful as a starter for those less experienced with grant writing.

- *EdPubs.* Available at www.edpubs.gov/

  Look in the product catalog on this website for free publications from the U.S. Department of Education that demonstrate successful projects and provide other information about department programs that may be useful for grant seekers.

- Karsh, E., & Fox, A. (2014). *The only grant-writing book you'll ever need* (4th ed.). New York: Basic Books.

This book provides exercises, resources, and interviews with funders that contain useful information for grant seekers.

Guided Practice

1. Review the proposal in Appendix 9-B. Use the guidelines in the chapter to explain what was done well, what needs work, and how the proposal exemplifies the chapter guidelines.
2. Write a paragraph about an idea you have for a service project. Look through the resources listed in this chapter to find one or more RFPs that might fit your idea.
3. Peruse books and websites about grant writing. Make a list of additional guidelines that you want to remember.

Reference

Noonoo, S. (February 10, 2015). The 9 essentials of crowdfunding for the classroom. *eSchool News.* Retrieved 22 August 2015 from www.eschool news.com/2015/02/10/crowdfunding-the-classroom-476/.

Request for Proposals

Funding of e-Learning Projects

The Offices of the Provost and Vice Provost for Undergraduate Education are offering financial support to teaching faculty to develop new courses and/or revise and upgrade existing e-Learning courses aimed at the teaching of on-campus students.

Eligibility

All full-time teaching faculty at all campuses.

Level and Duration of Support

We anticipate awards from $2500–$5000 per grant. We request that these funds be spent in one year after receiving the award.

What Is e-Learning?

Historically the term e-Learning has a number of meanings. For simplicity we adopt a pragmatic definition of an e-Learning course:

Any course with a significant online component. For sake of argument, 'significant' implies the online component is greater than 40%. The blended/hybrid/flipped/inverted formats are examples of the latter.

Goal

Here our goal is to encourage development, experimentation, and innovation in e-Learning based instruction by faculty by providing modest support for such. Support is limited to development of courses aimed at students enrolled on campus (this includes all campuses). It is our desire that these courses add significant value to undergraduate education, i.e., improved student learning, engagement, and retention.

Expectations

Our expectations include:

1. These courses would be for credit.
2. These courses should be substantive, in depth, of high quality, and challenging to the enrolled students. (Online lectures alone would not suffice.)
3. These courses should show an improvement (in student learning outcomes) over existing formats.
4. The development and production period should be timely with implementation of the course during the calendar year (spring, summer, or fall semesters).

Types of Activities Supported

The supported efforts might include (but are not limited to):

Conversion of existing traditional courses to e-Learning infused courses.

Dramatic improvement of student learning in existing e-Learning based courses.

Development of e-Learning units that would significantly enhance a traditional course by running in parallel with face-to-face labs/studios/field-trip types of activity.

In addition, critical remedial courses (here, noncredit courses would be appropriate) could be included.

New, previously untaught classes are not encouraged. In our opinion, the effort to develop and implement such undeveloped courses would require considerably more resources than currently available.

Proposal Applications

Please limit the proposal to 3–4 pages + budget page.

Application to Include

Description of the course with a brief summary of possible relevant e-Learning experiences from earlier efforts and from the literature.

Rationale for introducing e-Learning and predicted benefits to student learning.

Description of likely format and details of the proposed course components (online, face-to-face portions, Skype, etc.).

Description of the evaluation/assessment to be applied to the implemented course (guidelines and suggestions will be provided after awards are granted).

For major revisions of existing online courses, include a brief history of course, enrollment, and proposed changes in the course design.
Description and justification of how resources would be used to achieve success (i.e., budget justification).

Proposed Budget

Examples of items that might be requested:

- Funding of an assistant
- Software and equipment for production
- Purchase of online teaching materials (e.g., videos or online exercises)
- Copyright expenses
- Maintenance and/or implementation costs (with a projection of sustainability past the grant)
- Updating/revision costs

Requests for summer salary are discouraged. Matching funds from departments and deans are strongly encouraged.

Final Report to Include

A description of the course features that were developed and deployed including a course syllabus.
Results of course evaluations/assessments.
Plans for and likelihood of improvements/revision for future course offerings.

(For new e-Learning courses, a preliminary report is requested, followed by a final report to be submitted in a timely fashion.)

Review of Proposals

A subcommittee of the Teaching Academy will review the proposals and make their funding recommendations to the Vice Provost for Undergraduate Education.
Awards will be announced as soon as possible.

Proposal Submission and Due Date

Proposals may be submitted as PDF files by e-mail attachment. Again, please limit the written materials to 3–4 pages + budget page.

Questions

If you have questions, please contact the Teaching Academy Director.

College of Education
Faculty Funding Awards Proposal Cover Sheet

Submit Cover Sheet and Proposal (electronic copy) to Associate Dean for Research

Title of Proposal: *Exploring the role of technology use in developing resource-rich, student-centered instruction*

Acceptance of Conditions: Submission of this proposal electronically signals that we agree to adhere to the conditions for accepting a College of Education Faculty Funding Award as outlined in the call for proposals.

Brief Abstract of Proposed Project (250 Words Maximum)

We propose to continue the work of our @RiSC research team as it studies effective uses of technology in K–20 education.

Funding would help us to continue our current funded project and initiate another, as outlined below.

Currently, with funding from the College, T&L Department, Provost's Office, Smith Foundation, and Stubblefield Foundation, our team has established a flipped teacher education course and a video production lab for use by faculty and students who are interested in flipped instruction. Our work on flipped instruction has already resulted in three presentations and two refereed articles; more are in progress. Our exploration of technology-supported direct instruction will help us to provide educators not only with sound theoretical grounding for flipping their instruction but also with concrete guidelines to facilitate the technology-supported implementation of this strategy.

Second, to support interaction and provide just-in-time instruction during the in-class segment of flipped classrooms, we must understand which technologies can help learners across contexts and disciplines engage in learning. We plan to engage our teacher education students (BA and EdM) in this study by having them research applications and websites and study the effective, evidence-based classroom uses of these technologies. At the same time, we intend to integrate into our own classes theoretically and pedagogically sound technologies that can be used across contexts and disciplines, and we will explore student engagement and transfer based on the software use.

We hope to encourage others in the College and University to join us in these efforts.

Proposal Narrative
(Limited to 4 Pages)

Description of the Project

Aspect 1: Studying Teacher Conceptions of Engaging Direct Instruction

The @RiSC video production lab provides students and faculty with resources to create direct-instruction video support for flipped instruction (one instance of a potential resource-rich, student-centered [or RiSC] learning context). However, there are no real guidelines for the development and use of such videos across disciplines and learning contexts. Throughout the current semester and for summer and fall, we will collect data about what teacher education students and faculty believe that engaging direct instruction supported by technology looks like; each grade level, classroom, and disciplinary area has its own genre, expectations, standards, strategies, and content, so direct instruction can take many different forms and have a variety of challenges. Because engaging direct instruction is central to successful flipping, it is crucial to understand how teachers view this element so that we can prepare teacher education/professional development accordingly. Research questions include:

1. How do faculty and teacher education students define direct instruction?
2. What do participants see as challenges with creating and using direct instruction?
3. What factors contribute to perceived differences, if any, among disciplines and grade levels regarding direct instruction?
4. What do teacher education students perceive can make direct instruction engaging for students?
5. How do these perceptions change when technology is used to support direct instruction?
6. How do the direct instruction videos that participants make reflect their views of direct instruction?
7. What are the perceptions of K–12 and teacher education students to videos used in instruction?

At the same time, the research team faculty will participate in this study by constructing and investigating the use of videos for pre-service classes in Sped, EdTech, and ELL. Each of these classes will use flipped instruction, focusing specifically on learner engagement. Assessment of this part of our project will involve interviewing all participants about their understandings and experiences and evaluating video products using a rubric. In addition, we will ask our participants to show their videos to as many members of their target learner (K–12) populations as possible in order to evaluate user friendliness, comprehensibility, interest, and other aspects of engagement. Assessment of these constructs will be made using surveys and instruments that we have shown to have psychometrically sound properties for this examination. As a result, we hope to be able to provide educators not only with sound theoretical grounding for flipping their instruction but also with concrete guidelines to facilitate the technology-supported implementation of this strategy. The assessment scheme will allow us to improve instruction in the College of Education and support teacher education students in their quest to provide engaging instruction to their students. To help us to accomplish this study, funding is needed to make sure that the laboratory is staffed so that our participants have access and we can collect usage and product data.

Aspect 2: Studying Engagement and Transfer

At the same time that we are collecting data about engaging direct instruction and student engagement as outlined above, we will also work with our teacher education students to understand which additional technologies can help learners across contexts and disciplines engage in learning both in and outside of the classroom. As part of this @RiSC (flipped) project, we intend to model in our classes theoretically and pedagogically sound technologies that can be used across contexts and disciplines, and we will explore student engagement and knowledge transfer using instruments that we have constructed and used over the last two years. Our overall research question, as suggested by Garrett (1991/2009) and other researchers, is:

What kind of [technology], integrated how into what kind of syllabus, at what level of learning, for what kind of learners, is likely to be effective for what specific learning purpose(s)? The proposed participants in this project are graduate and under-graduate teacher education students (BA and EdM). These teacher education students will interact with K–12 students using the technologies they review and collect data around engagement and learning to help them deconstruct and answer the overall research question above. The principal data collec-tion will occur through self-report, interviews, and researcher observations. The study a priori analysis of power using an F-distribution sample size is 176 to detect .40 (large) effect.

Upon completion of both aspects of this project, we expect to have a robust model of effective flipped instruction, including strat-egies and technologies, to share with researchers and educators.

Rationale for the Project

The ultimate objective of our project is to create a model pro-gram for faculty and K–12 teachers across the nation to flip their instruction successfully and thereby improve student learning and engagement (Bergmann & Sams, 2012; Ruddick, 2012). Our overall theoretical foundation stems from the task engagement literature. Regardless of the context, the purpose of technology use in classrooms is to support learning. Learn-ing happens when teachers offer their learners engaging oppor-tunities (Csikszentmihalyi, 1990; Lin, 2012; Spolsky, 1989), regardless of the technology that exists. Engagement, in general, suggests that learners are deeply involved in a task. According to the literature, this requires learners to perceive themselves capable of the task, to see value, purpose, and use in the task, to be free from anxiety during the task, and to have appropriate and relevant feedback (Cambourne, 1995; Egbert, Hanson-Smith, & Chao, 2007; Meltzer & Hamman, 2004). Overall, an engaging task is authentic, meaningful, and doable for students; in other words, it provides a range of choices of resources and other task elements as part of student-centered instruction. Used well, technology can help support and provide engaging tasks for learners, regardless of whether it is cutting edge or not so new. Engaging tasks, Egbert (2010, p. 2) claims, can help teachers succeed in any technological context, but especially those where

> the use of any digital technology (i.e., old, new, computer, cell phone, calculator) makes [learning] more effective (leads to greater success by, for example, providing challenge, differentiating, supplying access to otherwise inaccessible interactions or data) and/or more efficient (speeds the rate of learning by, for example, allowing students and teachers to spend more time on effective tasks) in pursuit of whatever [goals], objectives, and standards are to be achieved.

We link this engagement framework to effective flipped instructional approaches, in which students work with direct-instruction materials outside of class and focusing on interactive, social activities to deepen content understanding during class time. Students watch teacher-created multimedia screencasts or podcasts of lectures and/or employ other direct-instruction materials and have access to diverse resources outside of school. The very brief online lectures can be assigned as homework or as direct instruction during lessons. In this way, students come to class ready to explore, elaborate, and interact around the content in ways that meet their needs more effectively than strictly seat time can (Bergman & Sams, 2012; Foertsch, Moses, Strikeweda, & Litzkow, 2002; Kim, Byun, & Lee, 2012; Strayer, 2007). This can improve student interest and performance, especially for those who traditionally underperform. In other words, the flipped classroom can be engaging to students, as teachers focus class time on discussion and hands-on activities to increase understanding and performance.

However, we understand that it is not enough just to expose colleagues and teacher education students to innovative teaching approaches and say "now you go do it." In order for teachers to transfer their learning to their current/future classrooms, they must both understand the evidentiary bases for effective approaches to teaching and learning and also be able to implement them. In other words, for transfer to occur the task must be authentic and adequately represented during initial instruction. This is particularly true for technology-based approaches, in which appropriate content, skills, technology, and strategies must be integrated in complex ways. Even more important, teacher education students themselves must be engaged by such approaches and experience their positive effects; this is one reason we see it as crucial to involve our pre-service teachers in this project.

To date, our team has addressed some of the needs noted above for engaging, student-centered learning in our elementary education program. The Methods of Teaching Special Education (TCH_LRN 470) and Introduction to ESL (TCH_LRN 413) courses have already been flipped and are under ongoing study. From this experience we have already begun to glean important guidelines that can help other faculty and provide a starting point for individual flips. Faculty funding will allow us to continue this interesting and necessary work.

Advancement of Strategic Plan(s)

Our research directly addresses two focal goals of the University's strategic plan:

- preeminent in research and discovery, teaching, and engagement.
- transformative educational experience to undergraduate students and continuing the development of a preeminent research portfolio.

Our project emphasizes cutting-edge instructional strategies that have garnered great interest not only across the university but throughout public education. In addition, our focus on undergraduate teacher education students meets the University's emphasis on transformative experiences. In developing a theoretical basis and practical guidelines for resource-rich, student-centered instruction, we are leading the field in both research and teaching. In the next step of this project, we intend to engage teachers around the region, thereby fitting this project perfectly within the University plan.

In the same ways, our project meets all of the goals in the College strategic plan, particularly Goals 1 and 2:

1. Achieve national and international preeminence in innovation, creativity, and the advancement of education and allied programs.
2. Provide a premier education and transformative experience that prepares students to excel in a global society.

In addition, our current publications and presentations on flipped instruction appear in premier outlets, which supports the College's quest for renown.

Timeline for Project

The Spring semester is being spent setting up the video production lab, acquainting people with its uses, and creating initial videos. New data collection will begin on an exploratory basis during Summer for both aspects of our project and will continue through Fall. While we continue (and perhaps revise) our data collection in Spring, we will also be analyzing data and sharing our results. We will share some of our preliminary results at a fall conference.

Plans for Manuscript(s) and/or External Funding Proposal(s)

From the excitement around the presentations and publications we have completed and the funding that we have already secured, we are sure that there is great interest in both the topic and content of our research. To support further study, our team has already begun crafting proposals for two fall competitions. We are preparing IES and NFS proposals, and any evidence we can gather through this Faculty Funding award project will help us not only secure the funding but plan effective teacher development.

In addition to individual and team manuscripts sent to practical and research journals (i.e., *AERJ, TTE, Exceptional Children*, etc.), we plan to co-author a book for Routledge that connects research, theory, and practice in flipped instruction. This text will be the seminal publication on evidence-based application of this strategy.

JL Stubblefield Trust/Bonnie and Clifford Braden Foundation Funding Proposal

Title of Proposal: *Helping teachers create resource-rich student-centered flipped learning: Focus on video production*

Brief Abstract of Proposed Project

This project aims to improve K–12 student learning and excitement about school with an innovative teaching technique called "flipped learning." In a flipped classroom, K–12 students work with rich direct-instruction materials outside of class, allowing them to focus on interactive, social activities that deepen understanding during class time. This is the opposite of a "traditional" classroom and can lead to greater student achievement. Our ultimate objective is to create a model program for teachers across the nation to flip their instruction successfully and thereby improve student learning and engagement (Bergmann & Sams, 2012; Ruddick, 2012). This project builds on our past work with flipped instruction strategies. Specific activities include: 1) building a video production lab at the WSU College of Education for use in all teacher education courses; 2) training pre-service teachers to create effective videos to flip their classrooms; 3) assisting pre-service teachers in implementing and evaluating flipped instruction. A grant from the Stubblefield Trust/Braden Foundation will allow us to directly increase the knowledge and skills of pre-service teachers by flipping their teacher education courses and also giving them hands-on experience in building the main component (videos) to flip their own instruction. The pre-service teachers will move their direct instruction in each disciplinary area from in-class lectures to engaging and compelling videos for their K–12 students.

Proposal Narrative

Almost a decade ago, Perlstein (2003) noted the drop in overall achievement that too many students experience, especially a lack of interest in math and science. Students report that they find math and science disconnected from real life and, as one student put it, "a fat waste of time" (p. 120). These trends are even more troubling in low–SES areas and for students whose native language is not English. Research shows that flipped classrooms help improve student achievement and interest in math and science.

Our previous (2012–13) explorations, funded by a CoE Faculty Funding Award and a Smith grant, show that classroom teachers need tools, materials, time, and expertise to support their exploration of flipped instruction. The teacher education program is an optimal time for pre-service teachers to learn about this strategy so they can try it in their future classrooms. However, video construction tools are necessary to help teachers develop the essential videos for use in flipped instruction. Support from the Stubblefield Trust/Braden Foundation will allow us to build these videos, evaluate results, and develop a model for use in teacher preparation programs throughout the nation.

Final Report Form for a State Grant

Final Report

Within 60 days of completing your project, submit a written report documenting the effectiveness of the project, providing the information indicated below.

1. Name of Institution:
2. Title of project:
3. Status of partnerships—List the partners that participated in this project:
4. Overview of project activities and extent to which they were accomplished:
5. Performance standards and extent to which they were met using performance measures**:
6. Contact hours:
7. Number of participants—Enter the total number of participants for each applicable type of participant, below:

Final Budget Report

List all project expenses for each partner, including leveraged monies (other funds that contributed to the project such as foundation, LEA, other federal funds).

Budget Summary
(limited to 1 page)

	Description	Amount
Salaries		
Wages		
Goods & Services		
Travel		
Benefits		
Equipment		
TOTAL		

Budget Narrative

Salaries
Wages
Goods & Services
Benefits
Equipment

10

WRITING REFERENCES AND OTHER SERVICE

From a letter of reference from an external file review:

> I appreciate the invitation to review the promotion and tenure file of Dr. X to Associate Professor. In preparation for this important task, I carefully read the materials provided to me that specify the expectations at X State for this advancement and then considered the materials for Dr. X in light of them and with ongoing reference to them. This review is independent of any personal or professional relationship with her.

Overview

This chapter covers an array of service opportunities not mentioned in other chapters in this book. It begins with a general description of responsibilities that these loosely linked service opportunities share and then turns to specific information for each type of service. Each of these specific sections includes the unique attributes of the service, the responsibilities of the person engaging in it, and, when appropriate, either a specific example of the service product or a location where an example can be obtained.

This chapter addresses:

- General responsibilities of service
- Guidelines for writing internal and external references
- Writing a column
- Consulting
- Curriculum development
- Guest editing or lecturing
- Membership in professional organizations
- The roles of technology in service
- Listing additional service on a CV or résumé

General Responsibilities of Service

From writing references to curriculum development, the varied service opportunities included in this chapter (like those in the rest of this book) require expertise around a clearly identifiable line of scholarship that results in recognition by the larger educational community. The invitational nature of the majority of these opportunities depends on a person's standing within an academic community. Membership in professional organizations solidifies areas of interest and serves as markers for others to understand the parameters of a person's scholarly pursuits. One responsibility, then, for a hopeful contributor to these service options comes with a need to consistently portray the range of knowledge and proficiencies the person holds. This strong and coherent knowledge base sets the stage for invitations to write references, vie for writing a column, engage in consulting work, develop curriculum, and compete for guest editorships and lecturer opportunities. These responsibilities also demand the need to communicate well in writing and speaking for various contexts. As true for many service obligations, they typically come with time frames and specific due dates. Therefore, a responsibility to meet submission deadlines provides another shared obligation. The differences across these options also bring chances to take service in various directions and add important chances for variety and creativity. However, a desire to diversify service tasks means that the service should still remain within a person's skills and time availability.

Writing Internal and External References

Writing references requires a careful and forthright consideration of a person's professional *competence* as evidenced by his or her accomplishments. Possessing a clear understanding of the concept of "competence" becomes an important first step; based on a systematic look at studies investigating competence for physicians but equally applicable to education and other fields, Epstein and Hundert (2002) propose this definition: "the habitual and judicious use of communication, knowledge, technical skills, clinical reasoning, emotions, values, and reflection in daily practice for the benefit of the individual and the community being served" (p. 226).

Provide Examples

Applying this definition of competence to education offers an important reminder that a well-rounded reference should blend an attention to expertise with a discussion of dispositions. It also suggests the importance of offering specific examples—in other words, taking an important attribute such as a person's knowledge and applying it to a specific situation. That is, flat statements (e.g., Stephen is an accomplished mathematician) are insufficient. The actions and products that support the statement need to immediately follow. For example, adding a statement that mentions Stephen's receipt of an award for early-career accomplishments within mathematics would move the comment from an ungrounded statement to one supported by evidence. This definition of competence provides a way to direct the content of the various types of references you might be asked to provide.

Link Attributes to Job or Position Requirements

The idea of writing a reference does not capture only a single type of service. Instead, writing references can take several directions. For those in the early years of their career, requests to write references for students quickly arise. Consider the example in Figure 10.1 written for a former graduate student (with pseudonyms) seeking a university position. For this type of reference, the author addresses the context for knowing Nate, the match between his doctoral program and the description of this position, the overall and unique aspects of Nate's experiences, and the personal attributes that would make him a valued colleague.

Beyond the blending of personal and academic accomplishments and attributes, a letter of reference should also evidence

Figure 10.1 Sample student reference letter.

Dear Dr. Harvey,

I have great pleasure in recommending Dr. Nate Jones for your consideration as an assistant professor in modern language education. I have known Nate since his doctoral days at X University, where I served as an instructor for several doctoral seminars that Nate took as well as a member of his dissertation committee. I have followed his career since his

Figure 10.1 (Continued)

graduation. I am very pleased that he is now seeking a return to the United States. As the following comments underscore, I think Nate holds many important qualities and experiences that link directly to your position.

First, Nate's doctoral program provided a background in literacy along with its attention to second language acquisition. In his dissertation, Nate focused on second language learning as does his recent work. However, he is well positioned to teach courses and work with graduate students across modern language acquisition and curriculum and instruction. In addition, and in part due to his work with Y, who has international recognition in the area of computer-assisted language learning, he has a rich understanding of technology and online instruction.

Second, Nate brings international experience to this role. Teaching abroad at the university level afforded Nate firsthand exchanges with people who learn a second language and pursue degrees that require a high level of academic English. In addition, this placed him in the role of living and working as a language learner. In combination, they set the stage for holding a deep grasp of the challenges and benefits that come from acquiring a language other than one's own. This provides an important experiential background to combine with his wealth of knowledge.

In addition, Nate has many personal attributes that will make him a valued colleague. He is a deep thinker and can make sense out of complexity—things that language learning demands. He is committed to his professional duties and is a responsible and productive contributor in collaborative endeavors.

In my final comments, I would like to return to Nate's academic accomplishments. Nate reads across domains and holds a flair for integrating these complex ideas into those that he can articulate and act upon. These dispositions and understandings will serve him well as a teacher who taps and models preferred practices, as a collaborator who works with

Figure 10.1 (Continued)

---

others to consider program development, and a scholar who shares this work with the educational community. I encourage you, and without hesitation, to carefully consider his application and its fit to your expectations. I know that if someone like Nate applied for a position at X University, our faculty would give him a favorable nod. Selecting a future colleague is an important task. I wish you well in your deliberations. Should I be of further help in your consideration of Nate or in commenting on Nate's match to your specific expectation, please feel free to contact me electronically (e-mail address) or by phone (home: xxx. xxx.xxxx, cell: xxx.xxx.xxxx).

Sincerely,
X, Ph.D.
Professor

---

the relationship between these pieces and the position under consideration. The example in Figure 10.2 shows how that can occur.

Appropriately linking comments in a review to the particulars of a position brings these important connections to the foreground rather than leaving them for inference by the search

Figure 10.2 Sample letter linking institutional requirements to student attributes.

To Whom It May Concern:

I am pleased to recommend Stephen Blumfield for your tenure-track appointment to teach adult learners, participate in service, and collaborate with colleagues to promote the various missions of your college. I know Stephen as his

Figure 10.2 (Continued)

instructor for several literacy courses and as a member of his dissertation committee. From these exchanges, I have developed very positive opinions about Stephen as a person, scholar, and future member of a college faculty. After reading about your college and the particulars of this position, I consider Stephen especially suited for your position. My following comments provide specific support for this stance.

Of importance, Stephen exceeds the educational expectations for this position. At this time, Stephen is ABD but is making good progress toward his intention to defend his dissertation by May. In addition to holding this advanced degree (a Ph.D. in literacy) before the start of this appointment, his course work, dissertation, and other doctoral experiences further align with your expectations. For example, Stephen's dissertation places him in collaboration with adult learners. While his work occurs with teachers, I would expect the understandings that he has gleaned from interacting with them would serve him well as he interacts with college students. Stephen also has experience with undergraduates, both as a teaching assistant and as an organizer and participant in a cyber-tutoring program that provided services to K–12 students in rural areas. His course work and dissertation also apply to developing college students' literacy. First, his course work included an assessment and instruction course, which I taught. In it, Stephen learned how to conduct assessments and use them to design intervention plans. His dissertation's focus on mathematical literacy also provides important understandings for teaching a college reading course. College students often have difficulty negotiating the literacy demands of various subject areas. While Stephen's course work in content area reading alerts him to these wider challenges, his dissertation provides a deep understanding of the

Figure 10.2 (Continued)

relationships between literacy and mathematics. Finally, Stephen participated in a seminar for teaching assistants, which I also taught. This provided opportunities to explore those overarching topics that apply to teaching at the college level. Beyond these overlays with the specific requirements for this position, Stephen has many personal qualities that make him a candidate to consider. They especially apply to his service obligations and the expectation for collaboration. Of importance, Stephen does not dodge hard work. He willingly gives his time and energy to projects—those that he initiates (like a community tutoring program that he organized while a full-time doctoral student) and those that he has the opportunity to join (like the cyber-tutoring project directed by Dr. X that I previously mentioned). I am confident that he would quickly become an integral member of your college and the expected commitment of all faculty members to community, teaching, and service. Further, Stephen is conscientious and dependable. He can be counted on to meet obligations in a timely and complete fashion. And he does so while maintaining goodwill and a smile. As this last comment suggests, Stephen has a personable way. He easily interacts with a range of students and faculty. His pleasant and professional demeanor will serve him well in the various roles that a faculty member assumes and the teaching and service expectations of this position. In combination, these personal attributes will make him a valued and productive colleague.

Clearly, I think Stephen warrants your consideration and highly recommend him for it. Should I be of further assistance in exploring the fit between Stephen's experiences and your needs, feel free to contact me by phone (xxx.xxx.xxxx) or electronically (e-mail inserted).

Sincerely,
X, Ph.D.
Professor, Literacy Education

committee members. The excerpt in Figure 10.3, written for the same student, Stephen, but for a different position, offers wording for another way to connect to the job's specifications. This example brings in specific activities that form links between Stephen's background and this job's expectations. These links are not left to chance but directly explained.

Consider Reference Requirements

As a person's career advances, invitations to serve as an external reviewer for candidates for promotion and tenure at other institutions will develop. As with other service opportunities, this will evolve from personal accomplishments and visibility and esteem in a wider professional community. Completing an external review comes with unique requirements. Instead of connecting a review to a job description, an external review must link to a university's promotion and tenure requirements; the invitation letter will specify the expectations. The letter in Figure 10.4, with pseudonyms inserted, provides an example of an invitation to

Figure 10.3 Alternate wording of a reference letter.

Finally, a candidate should fit the job description. Of initial importance, Stephen's interests and experiences coincide with the specialty areas that you note. He has worked with a STEM literacy project that involves collaboration with engineering and literacy education faculty. This opportunity sparked his interest in mathematical literacy. His dissertation combines these areas, working with teaching fellows to understand the infusion of mathematical literacy into their teaching context. As a teaching assistant, Stephen received experience teaching undergraduate students. His work with the teaching fellows extended his experiences to practicing teachers. His cyber-tutoring involvement provided experience with supervising tutors and making the arrangements for their tutoring sessions.

serve as an external reviewer. It provides the background of the person under consideration, the documents linked to the review, and the guidelines expected for the completion of this review.

Figure 10.4 Letter of invitation to write an external review.

Dear Professor X,

Thank you for agreeing to review and evaluate the scholarly work of Dr. William Hurd, who is seeking promotion to the rank of professor. As chair of the Tenure and Promotion Committee of the Department of Instruction and Teacher Education, I would appreciate receiving an electronic copy of your letter of evaluation with your signature as well as a 1- to 2-page summary of your curriculum vita by *January 30.* Please e-mail your letter and vita or biographical outline to (e-mail address provided).

Please use the attached unit criteria to guide your evaluation of Dr. Hurd's scholarship and research. The committee would also appreciate a statement describing your relationship, if any, with this candidate. Please be advised that the university cannot guarantee the confidentiality of letters prepared by external referees. The university will maintain the confidentiality of your letter to the extent allowed by (State) law (Provost letter, 5/4/95).

In this e-mail, you will find:

- Our departmental/unit tenure and promotion criteria
- A personal statement from the candidate, vitae, and selection of scholarly products

In your letter of evaluation *on your university's letterhead,* please include:

- A statement describing your relationship, if any, with this candidate
- Your evaluation of the candidate's scholarship and research in relationship to the enclosed criteria

Figure 10.4 (Continued)

Also please include:

• A 1- to 2-page summary of your curriculum vita or a brief
  biographical outline to acquaint Tenure and Promotion Committee members with your qualifications as a
  nationally recognized referee.

Thank you for your critically important contribution to our
review process.

Sincerely,

Dr. X, Tenure and Promotion Committee Chair
Department of Instruction and Teacher Education

The information and instructions in the letter need to be
carefully considered by the potential reviewer before agreeing
to write a letter that depends on it.

The letter in Figure 10.5, submitted by an external reviewer,
offers an example for linking a candidate's accomplishments to
promotion and tenure expectations. The ongoing return to the
invitation letter and promotion and tenure guidelines form a
base for this reviewer's efforts.

Another external review letter can be found in this chapter's
appendix. It provides an additional example of the guidelines
mentioned previously.

Be on Time

The time sensitivity of a promotion and tenure review process
makes submitting a letter by its due date extremely important
(and a professional courtesy). Due dates also matter for letters
written for students.

Figure 10.5 External review letter.

Dear Dr. X,

I am pleased to contribute to the important task of the consideration of the promotion of Dr. Y to full professor at Z University. I know Dr. X through our affiliation and leadership roles within the Association of XXX. Of importance for this review, we do not interact beyond attendance at XXX's annual conference. As requested, my response exclusively examines Dr. Y's scholarship. I carefully read and noted the scholarship expectations explained in the document sent to me to prepare for this task. I then examined his materials in light of my understanding of those expectations. I considered his accomplishments that followed his promotion to associate professor. I focus my comments on the standards noted for scholarship and the definitional attributes linked to them: consistent productivity that evidences quantity and quality. I begin with a discussion of consistency and quantity and then address quality. I end with a brief summary of my points.

Based on Dr. Y's vita and under the heading of Research and Scholarship, between 2001 and today, Dr. Y cites 26 publications (four of which are in press) in refereed journals. This results in an average of two refereed pieces per year. He separates a publication in the Yearbook from this list, but it, too, is a refereed outlet. The list of products indicated for scholarship at Z University also includes books. Dr. Y has one book scheduled for publication in 2013, which he co-authored with XXX. He notes two additional books (2001, 2008) under the heading of Creative Works. These books are written for young audiences. These publications might be classified as improving the education of students' spirits or enhancing the quality of people's life—areas cited in the scholarship narrative. Grants are also noted as products of scholarship. Dr. Y acquired several small grants, with the largest ($14,350)

Figure 10.5 (Continued)

funded by the X Center for International Studies. Beyond the receipt of one small grant, no listed products (refereed publications, books, technical reports) are noted between 2005 and 2007. This gap in productivity might come with an explanation that these documents do not offer. Those contextual considerations, if appropriate to bear in mind, can best be determined by a local consideration of known extenuating circumstances that might account for this gap. However, it perhaps calls into question an expectation for consistent productivity, the language used in the scholarship narrative.

At Z University, several areas contribute to quality: peer review, the reputation of the publication outlets, and their selectivity. Dr. Y's forthcoming book will be published by Pearson, a highly regarded outlet for academic texts. All of Dr. Y's journal outlets meet the expectation for peer review. Their reputation and overall quality waver. Dr. Y most often cites *RWT* (10 selections). These include brief essays (1–2 pages) on an array of topics. Seemingly, *RWT* was a previous name for *Reading Today*, a magazine-type publication of the International Reading Association. The widest readership of his selected journals comes from *The Reading Teacher*, a highly regarded practitioner journal also published by the International Reading Association. The *Journal of Reading Education* is published by the Organization of Teacher Educators in Reading, a group again linked to the International Reading Association. Dr. Y has one publication in this journal, which many well-known scholars use as an outlet for their work. *Reading Psychology* (five manuscripts) and *Literacy Research and Instruction* (four manuscripts) hold more visibility and higher regard within the literacy community as places to publish empirical work. With Dr. Y's literacy focus, his choice of journals linked to major professional organizations (e.g., IRA and ALER) as well as a selective journal that focuses on research is both reasonable and productive in the dissemination of his work. He has two publications in *Religious Education*, an outlet suited for

Figure 10.5 (Continued)

the expectation at Z University to "serve God and humanity."
The remaining journals, *Journal of College Reading and Learning*
and *Lectura*, seem appropriate choices for the substance of these
submissions (one in each). Immediately apparent in Dr. Y's work is his record of
multi-authored manuscripts. While Z University's scholarship
explanation does not directly address this issue, group versus
individual authorship often warrants attention. Collaboration
holds many advantages in keeping with X University's scholarship expectations such as the increased possibility of learning
from colleagues. Interactions during the collaborative writing
process also directly subject an individual's contribution to the
criticism and feedback of immediate peers rather than a dis-
tanced editorial board. I found no language in X University's
scholarship language that would problematize the preponder-
ance of Dr. Y's multi-authored work.

Dr. Y's vita notes many types of publications that fall outside of those directly listed as acceptable products for scholarship. Presentations at national and international conferences
are but one example. While not directly counted as products
for promotion, these additional activities might serve to evidence his overall activity within the literacy community and
his visibility across a range of venues and audiences. This is
in keeping with Z University's intention for scholars to "be
learners" and "contribute to the expansion of truth."

In summary, the number of products that Dr. Y has produced seems in keeping with Z University's standard for
quantity. However, the break in his publication record remains
a concern for "consistent productivity," and the number of
publications in less influential outlets impact the attribute of
quality, specifically the 10 publications in *RWT*. Two points
warrant mentioning in regard to this point. Especially in these
competitive times when more and more institutions demand
publication, most scholars have an ebb and flow to the outlets

Figure 10.5 (Continued)

> for their work. Of note for Dr. Y, the majority of his pieces in *RWT* come immediately after his last promotion. More recent publications exhibit a higher standard of quality and a clear focus on empirical work. In the end, I am drawn to the medley of contributions that define Dr. Y's scholarship.
>
> I consider the decisions for promotion and tenure important and difficult. I hope that the committee members and administrators left to make a final judgment for Dr. Y find my comments helpful during their deliberations. Should I be of additional service, feel free to contact me electronically (e-mail contact) or by phone (cell: xxx.xxx.xxxx).
>
> Sincerely,
> (Reviewer), Ph.D.
> Professor

In short, guidelines for writing reference letters include:

- address a candidate's professional and personal attributes
- link them to the position or review criteria
- attend to due dates
- review the letter for clarity, organization, and the accurate use of print conventions
- provide a letter with a professional appearance through the use of letterhead

Writing a Column

Another important way to provide professional service is writing a column, which sometimes involves serving as a section editor to provide oversight for an ongoing inclusion in a professional journal; at other times, writing a column can stem from a one-time invitation. As with other service opportunities, the possibility for writing a column begins by linking a column's orientation to your background, interests, and availability. For some journals, columns are divided into departments. Many journals have editors for their various columns or departments. For example, *Language Arts*, a publication of the National Council of Teachers of English (NCTE), has editors for three areas: Research and Policy, Professional Book Reviews, and Children's Literature Reviews (writing for the latter two was addressed in Chapter 4). Sample columns include those by Fisher and Frey (2015) and Hermann-Wilmarth and Ryan (2015). If this organization and these areas coincide with your interests and experiences, the process for applying must be understood. To distribute information about applying for a column editorship, some organizations place an advertisement in the journal that houses it or on their website. Potential editors can scan an organization's website to obtain specific direction for how to proceed. Carefully reading published columns and using them for exemplars and mentor texts provides a process for understanding the format and content of columns identified as targets for submission. The potential editor's institution's promotion and tenure policies would determine the level of prestige that comes with a column editorship.

Consulting

Consulting can include providing professional service for local school districts (e.g., professional development, discussed in Chapter 8), state departments of education, or other institutions of higher education both in the United States and abroad. These opportunities might come with or without compensation. Should compensation be received, a university's policies provide guidelines that explain the conditions that accompany these opportunities. If done during the academic year, most universities limit the amount of consulting a faculty member can do and have a reporting system for it. More flexibility often exists if consulting is completed during an off-contract period such as summer break. The content and format for a consulting opportunity is typically mutually agreed upon by the person offering the service and the organization seeking it. For example, some faculty members receive requests to offer their expertise to a committee working to reorganize licensure standards. Others contract with a local school or even international organizations to provide professional development across a period of time. (Appendix 10-B provides a letter of invitation to consult for the U.S. State Department overseas.) Still others provide their expertise to a range of stakeholders without an expectation for compensation. A careful consideration of the type of consulting and the conditions surrounding it (topic, dates, length, and remuneration) should occur prior to solidifying a consulting possibility.

Curriculum Development

Most faculty and some graduate students are involved in curriculum development by creating, editing, and updating the classes they teach. Many institutions also have committees that work with the development of curriculum or the approval of programmatic curricula. Curriculum development grants, both internal and external, are currently popular sources of support for developing online and other innovative curricular solutions. All these options might be considered not only for the institutional rewards they carry; at times, curriculum development accompanies and boosts a research agenda as developers collect empirical data to evidence the appropriateness of a certain curricular orientation for students' achievement. Other types of curriculum development link to a person's teaching as he or she diligently strives to keep a course and a program up to date; these changes and their outcomes can be documented for publication. Other curriculum development occurs with an entrepreneurial and profit-driven orientation, sometimes supported by federal grants in cooperation with international agencies. Like other service options, a person interested in curriculum development should carefully ponder the direction to take, the cost and benefits that accompany it, and the possibility of unintended consequences.

Guest Editing or Lecturing

Guest editing for a professional journal involves the same service opportunities previously explained in Chapter 3. The one exception is its temporary time period. Guest editors often serve for a themed issue for which they hold exceptional acknowledgment for their expertise. Lecturing, too, is invitational based on a person's status within an educational community or for a specific field of study. Often, guest lecturers hold an international reputation and the invitations come from an international venue. This sometimes involves a university. Being involved in these types of opportunities depends on having one's background and accomplishments known and valued. Your research and teaching accomplishments need to receive national and international attention—and quality service in other areas can help establish it.

Membership in Professional Organizations

Simply stated, memberships tend to define who one is as a member of an academic community. Therefore, intentionally select them to provide a sketch of your professional interests. As discussed in other chapters, a person would not join the

Association of Middle Level Education without a vested interest in that age group. A person who joins the International Literacy Association evidences a concern for the advancement of reading and writing, while joining the National Council of Teachers of Mathematics indicates a focus on mathematics. For many academics, the collection of memberships evidences the varied nature of their work. For example, a literacy person might apply that body of knowledge to science, technology, engineering, and mathematics (STEM) and to the teaching profession. This person's memberships would reflect the cross-disciplinary nature of their professional priorities. Of importance, professional membership is a first step in engaging in most aspects of professional service. Almost without exception, an organization reserves its service opportunities for its members.

The Roles of Technology in Service

Basic contributions of technology (the benefits of word processing systems, the use of search engines to find information, and the exchange of information) continue to apply to the service options mentioned here. For example, few, if any, institutions or organizations will accept a job or tenure reference that is not typed, and many require letters to be submitted online. Likewise, journal columns are word processed, and links to resources might require hypertext markup language (html). Further, using platforms such as Google Docs can simplify collaboration around curriculum development and resource presentation for consulting or guest lecturing. To provide effective service, the ubiquity of technology needs to be considered and its affordances invoked regularly.

Listing Additional Service on a CV or Résumé

The example in Figure 10.6 covers various types of service included in this chapter. As with most other service options, no mandated format exists. Therefore, these examples offer samples that can be modified. An important idea to remember is to maintain the basic format of the overall CV or résumé; in other words, the use of indentation, font, bold, italics, and spacing should be consistent across the document, with multiple entries under a heading arranged chronologically or alphabetically.

Figure 10.6 Sample service entries.

In-Service Presentations

2015   Upton Middle School, Farmington, NM
     Differentiation and Assessment: A Potentially Powerful Duo

2014   Lincoln Middle School, Miami, FL
     Reading in the Disciplines

2013   Elkton Middle School, San Diego, CA
     Middle Level Readers: From Evidence to Action

     Elkton Middle School, San Diego, CA
     Assisting Middle Level Readers: Knowledge about Intervention

Professional Memberships

American Educational Research Association
Association for Childhood Education International
International Reading Association
National Conference for Research on Language and Literacy

Professional Activities

Guest Lectures

2014   Mahidol University (Bangkok), Thammassat University (Bangkok), and Mae Fah Luang University (Chiang Rai) concerning: 1) qualitative research practices and

Figure 10.6 (Continued)

> perspectives, 2) publications and building a career path, and 3) language testing and assessment in the 21st century
>
> **External Reviews**
>
> 2014   University of South Carolina
> 2013   Indiana University
> 2013   Ohio University
> 2013   George Mason University
> 2013   Clemson University
>
> **Guest Reviews**
>
> 2014   *Review of Educational Research*
> 2013   *Elementary School Journal*
>
> **Administrative Service**
>
> 2007–2010   NCATE Board of Examiners
> 1997–1998   Member, Executive Council for drafting Delaware's Middle Level English Language Arts Standards
> 1987–1988   Member, writing team for State of Washington's Reading Curriculum Guidelines

Notice the consistency in spacing and content across entries; as noted throughout this book, these are crucial elements in creating a readable and effective vita.

Conclusion

Although one's background, interests, and time availability might intervene, service can occur. The range of options noted in this chapter affirms the diversity of choice available for those interested in participating in professional service in education. These options also confirm the need for faculty and students to develop a professional identity that establishes credibility within an identified educational community. The most important attribute is a willingness to get started—to make a choice, set a goal, make a plan, and enjoy the many personal and professional benefits service affords.

Recommended Resources

- Miller, R. I. (1987). *Evaluating faculty for promotion and tenure.* San Francisco, CA: Jossey-Bass.

  This text would best be used by selecting the sections that apply and extrapolating information from them. The book's organization makes it easy to make these choices.

- Glatthorn, A. A., Boschee, F., & Whitehead, B. M. (2005). *Curriculum leadership: Development and implementation.* Thousand Oaks, CA: Sage Publications.

  This text applies to an interest in service within curriculum development. It can provide insights about topics to address and ways to do so.

- Perkmann, M., & Walsh, K. (2008). Engaging the scholar: Three types of academic consulting and their impact on universities and industry. *Research Policy, 37*(10), 1884–1891.

  If interested in engaging in consulting, this text can offer guidance through its explanation of different types of consulting, what they entail, and what they offer.

Guided Practice

1. Select a journal you regularly read that includes columns. Select the option best suited for your interests and read a column to better understand its specific attributes. Repeat this process for two to three journals to understand their

shared and unique features—from length to tone. Armed with this information, write a column for submission.

2. As you approach a third year or promotion and tenure review period, write a letter of reference for yourself. Use this letter not only to practice writing a review but also to objectively evaluate the relationship between your accomplishments and the expectations noted for them. Give yourself sufficient time to further support strengths and take steps to rectify gaps. External reviews should not come as a surprise, and this task, if done well, will avoid it.

3. Practice writing a student reference with yourself or someone you know as the "student." What are the strengths and weaknesses of this student? How will you express these to the benefit of both the student and the hiring organization?

References

Epstein, R. M., & Hundert, E. M. (2002). Defining and assessing professional competence. *JAMA, 287*(2), 226–235.

Fisher, D., & Frey, N. (2015). Teacher modeling using complex informational texts. *The Reading Teacher, 69*(1), 63–69.

Hermann-Wilmarth, J. M., & Ryan, C. L. (2015). Doing what you can: Considering ways to address LGBT topics in language arts curricula. *Language Arts, 92*(6), 436–443.

Dear X,

I appreciate the invitation to review the promotion and tenure file of Dr. X to Associate Professor. In preparation for this important task, I carefully read the materials provided to me that specify the expectations at X State for this advancement and then considered the materials for Dr. X in light of them and with ongoing reference to them. This review is independent of any personal or professional relationship with her.

Before directly commenting on Dr. X's work in light of the expectations for her, one observation assumes importance: Dr. X's use of *we* in her personal overview of her work. While the promotion and tenure guidelines specifically note the appropriateness of "teamwork and other collaborative relationships," it also notes a responsibility to clarify the "candidate's role in the joint effort." Especially given the shifts in collaborators that occur across Dr. X's work and her placement in the list of authors, providing a clear explanation of these various collaborations would have been helpful.

Dr. X separates her scholarship into three "lanes." While she provides labels that capture these areas, the more important explanation of the coherency across them is less clear. She states that they connect and build upon initial work, but her various explanations of the areas remain relatively boxed in their own silos. This leaves it to a reader to infer their relationships and coherency—a task that moves from verifying a person's claims to framing them. Scholars certainly construct and reconstruct the direction of their work and change areas of emphasis. Dr. X states that this occurred in her career. The expectation remains to use her personal statement to assist evaluators to "interpret the extent, balance, and scope of the faculty member's scholarly achievements." One clear direction for her work is an attention to second-language acquisition. She consistently, and without exception, links her professional activities to this important area.

In specifically addressing research activity, the promotion and tenure guidelines reference "depth, duration, and/or persistence." Since arriving at X State in 2009, and I base my evaluation from that time period, Dr. X has published five book chapters and has two in preparation. Two chapters appeared in the same text, and most were published outside the United States. All were collaborative efforts, with Dr. X taking the lead on one. She published one article in a refereed journal (2010) and has three under review and one in preparation. These, too, were done in collaboration. She rounds these products out with one encyclopedia entry (2013) and two conference proceedings (both in 2011). In addition to these published works, she notes 16 conference presentations between 2010 and 2013. They include local (two), regional (one), national (seven), and international (six) venues. As with her published works, she did these presentations with colleagues, assuming the lead on five. Without explanation from Dr. X, understanding her contribution to these publications and presentations remains unclear. However, alphabetizing (which suggests equal contribution) does not seem to apply. Adding a qualitative look at the selected outlets also contributes to understanding their potential impact. The selection of outlets provides one way to do this analysis. Here, her choices waver. Her one peer-reviewed journal publication appears in a practitioner journal. Her articles under review are in more well-known and established journals such as *TESOL Journal* and *Linguistics and Education*. The publishers for the books containing her book chapters generally lack name recognition. Her conference presentations range from NCTE, which has wide membership and outreach, to a conference titled Task-Based Learning and Teaching. According to a Google search, these "international task-based language teaching conferences aim to bring together researchers and educators with interests in tasks and task-based language teaching." This intention seems to coincide with Dr. X's work but is not a household name. In summary, these products align with the options noted in the promotion and tenure guidelines and serve to "validate and communicate" her scholarship. However, having a more uniform record of ongoing productivity and a more distinguished (or explained) selection of outlets would further contribute to the potential impact of her publications and presentations.

Dr. X clearly evidences the quality of her teaching and the wide range of her service. Both are laudable. She consistently received high rankings on student evaluations with a teaching load that sometimes exceeded a 2/2 assignment. She also taught a variety of courses and supervised student teachers. These contextual factors all add a sense of awe for her consistently high level of accomplishments in teaching. Her level of service evidences a characterization of a faculty member who is a good citizen at home and an important contributor to her professional community. Teaching and service matter, and she attends to both with a high level of success. Both lay claim to time. As previous comments suggest, her specific scholarship accomplishments are less remarkable. However, a differently framed explanation in her personal statement might have allowed a more favorable view of her accomplishments in terms of "magnitude and quality" (and she is not without some indication of both). Of importance in considering the added expectation of "a high likelihood of sustained contributions," she notes plans for the future and upcoming changes in the conditions of her workload. These facts bode well for a more sustained and improved level of research activity.

To summarize, I turn to Dr. X's position responsibility statement. It holds her to "sustain a program of research that leads to publication in refereed books, journals, and other publications, as well as presentations at professional conferences." She attended to each piece. She also met the requirement of the ___ Department of Education. Her teaching and service are stellar. Her ongoing collaboration with a variety of colleagues (including students) attests to her collegiality. Everything, however, is on balance. Those closer to X State who better grasp its promotion and tenure guidelines and hold firsthand knowledge of their specific application are best positioned to make that final determination. I hope that my comments contribute in a helpful way to that important decision.

In keeping with the cover letter that accompanied Dr. X's, I have attached a current and abbreviated vita as well as a short bio. Should I be of further assistance, please feel free to contact me by phone (work: xxx.xxx.xxxx; mobile: xxx.xxx.xxxx) or electronically (e-mail address).

Sincerely,
(Name)
Professor
College of X
X University
City, State

Letter of Invitation to Consult From the U.S. State Department (edited)

I am contacting you with a proposal for cooperation based on the recommendation of our Regional EL Officer.

We at the Public Affairs section of the US Embassy have received special funding to organize a project we call TEACHER TECH CAMP.

Funding for this "Teacher Tech Camp" project will allow us to organize a series of workshops for elementary and secondary school teachers in all 14 regions of [our country] with the goal of promoting and enhancing the use of technology and digital resources in the English language classroom. This project will reach up to 300 teachers and trainers (ca 20 per region, 14 regions) and teacher trainers in a priority field—for both [our] and US governments—the strengthening of knowledge of English language in [our] population.

Project Description

This professional development project will focus on use of technology and digital resources in English language classrooms and will give teachers of English training in the use of modern teaching methods to comply with the growing demands on language training. Teachers are hungry for this type of training, basically to allow them to get ahead of their students in terms of technical skills. This project will consist of two rounds (around one month each) of regional workshops organized in cooperation with local teacher training centers. The project will be implemented with Minister of Education support so that completion of the seminar could be registered as professional development and awarded by an appropriate certificate.

The project should fulfill the following criteria: must reach out to a representative number of schools across the [country]; must be worthwhile for teachers, sustainable and able to be repeated in the future; offer useful information in a reasonable timeframe which would ensure sufficient exposure to the topic (knowledge acquired in the workshops must be sufficiently fostered); must be beneficial for career development of participating teachers. In the interest of sustainability, one of the initial sessions will target teacher trainers who already have worked in similar thematic areas. Those trainers will be able to carry on the project in the future to ensure a sufficient multiplier effect.

Logistics: 14 two-day workshops for 20 teachers each, should offer both classroom instruction (ca 8 hrs) and practical skill building. The specific themes for the workshops will be developed by the U.S. trainers in advance, in cooperation with [in-country] partners. Computers or iPads with internet connectivity will be used during instruction. At a maximum two participants can share an iPad.

Realistically, we envision covering 2 regions per week which amounts to total of 7 weeks of training, roughly 2 x 1 month of trainer's time (or a bit less) within the 1st half of the year. Sufficient time for training content development for the US trainer should be built in. The training will be organized in two waves, and could, but need not be carried out by two different trainers.

Materials used in the projects should be recommended/developed by the potential trainers and should include the American English website and related resources.

We would like to ask you whether you would be interested in becoming one of the trainers of the project. It means that you would come to [our country] for roughly a month of teacher training in various regions of the country. The funding we have available would ensure similar financial conditions as are offered by the English Language Specialist program. The grants to trainers will be issued—most likely—through Fulbright.

I am writing to you in agreement with [the] Cultural Attaché who is my supervisor and project leader on our side.

I am ready to answer any questions you may have in connection with this project. We are in its initial stage, and there is space for modifications, changes, and improvements.

Thank you for considering this possibility, and look forward to hearing from you.

Index